INVINCIBLE

A 40-DAY JOURNEY TO INCREASE YOUR CONFIDENCE IN GOD

JAKE MCCANDLESS & RITA HALTER THOMAS

STAND FIRM
RESOURCES

Copyright © 2019 by Jake McCandless

Distributed by Ingram Spark

Published by Stand Firm Books www.standfirmministries.com

General Editor Dr. Angela Ruark
with Stand Firm Books

A Spiritual Preparedness Resource
Spiritual Preparedness Devotional #1

ISBN: 978-0-578-56459-3

For the hope that you STAND FIRM.

TABLE OF CONTENTS

Week 1
VICTORY

Week 2
PROVISION

Week 3
PROTECTION

Week 4
IMPOSSIBLE

Week 5
BEYOND

Week 6
IN THE END

ACKNOWLEDGMENTS

I don't just simply sit down to write and then everything flows. It's more of a war for me to get words on a page and a project completed. I also tend to work like a mad scientist, which can be dangerous for those near the lab. Devotionals for *Invincible* began to float around in the fall of 2015. Many hands touched the early ones and helped them become what you're about to read. I can't even begin to thank everyone, but I'm going to try.

My wife, Amanda, and daughters, Andrea and Addie, get the first thank-you. Amanda's gone to great lengths to allow me to write and share the message of Stand Firm Ministries. She's put up with a lot and worked hard to let me have time to write. Thank you for taking the wild steps and going to great lengths to help this message get out there. I may get my name on the book, but you'll get the crown in the kingdom.

Andrea and Addie are at an outing without their Daddy tonight because he's playing on his computer (AKA writing this). I hope more than anything that these words make it into their hearts, and they stand firm. I also hope that, one day, they know that this writing stuff wasn't in vain.

Next, is the rest of my family: Mom, Dad, Kylie, Jesse, Poppa, Nana, Rodney, Melinda, and down the line—thank you all for your support and caring about this endeavor.

Along the line of supporters, thank you to all who support Stand Firm Ministries. Also, a big thank-you to the congregations I've pastored while on this project: Mount Vernon Baptist Church, Endtime.Church, and Turner Street Baptist Church. You've dealt with a busy pastor and have shown so much support. To Christopher Mantei especially, thank you for stepping in and carrying Endtime.Church on your shoulders during this extensive project.

On the writing end, none of this would be possible without my agent, Cyle Young, of Hartline Literary Agency. You've gone to great lengths on my behalf and have fought for me. My co-author, Rita Halter Thomas, has almost been the ghostwriter for me over the past four years. She's edited everything I've done. I'm glad she's getting her name rightfully on the cover, and I look forward to working with her on the second devotional in this series. Also, Dr. Angela Ruark, along with her husband Bill, have been cracking the whip, moving the Stand Firm Books train ahead. As the general editor for Stand Firm Books, Angela served as proofreader and final editor for this book. And a shout-out to Cherrilynn Bisbano, Cindy Sproles, the Blue Ridge Mountain Christian Writers Conference, Serious Writers, Inc., writers of the numerous publishing house rejection letters, and everyone else who had a hand in shaping this book.

INTRODUCTION

A young shepherd boy walked onto the plain, armed only with a sling and five stones, to face an undefeated giant; one warrior picked up a donkey's jawbone to defeat 1,000; a general led 300 men against an army of 135,000. Although each person was seemingly outnumbered and overmatched, all marched forward with a swagger and staggering confidence. The swagger and staggering confidence, in their God who sent them, baffled the onlookers and odds-makers. With unflinching obedience, these, who appeared to be underdogs, walked away—each with a dominant and definite victory.

A government official was thrown into a pit of lions for praying; three young men were sentenced to be burned alive because they didn't bow; a disciple was boiled in a vat of oil for preaching. All of them were given ultimatums and threatened. All were fully aware that their bold stances for God placed their lives at risk. They flinched not. They remained faithful. Their heads were held high even when led to their fates. Each told their executioners that their God could save them.

These men appeared invincible.

And they were invincible—not because of their own strength or ability, but because they belonged to and followed an Invincible God.

The same God you and I belong to and follow.

1

Therefore, like them and because of Him, we're invincible, too.

You may not believe that God can and will impart His invincibility upon you to carry out your calling and your walk with Him. That's why this book was written.

You may not face life's challenges with the swagger and staggering confidence that come from knowing that the unseen hand guiding you is stronger than any visible hand you'll ever encounter. But you can get there. You need to get there. Again, this is the reason for this book.

Invincible is a 40-day journey—or maybe it's better described as a 40-day workout. We want to build up your faith muscles. We want to strengthen your belief in God. We want to fortify your confidence in the God who is invincible. There's no better way to reframe your outlook on life than remembering what God has already done. His works display a God fully capable of bringing us through whatever fire we may face. Whether that fire is a health crisis, a relationship crisis, a financial difficulty, a step of faith, a task, or a specific calling—whatever it is you're facing or will face—you can be confident that God will bring you through. His path isn't always easy, but it's the right path and it's the best path.

You need this 40-day journey. So, welcome to *Invincible*.

A Welcome from Jake

I can't thank you enough for choosing *Invincible*. Not because of my part in writing it, but because it tells me you're serious about your faith. Your book selection tells me you're concerned about being ready for the challenges that lie ahead in your life. Your purchase shows you're making a real commitment to spend devotional time with God for 40 days. That's what really excites me. You're not just reading a book, you're meeting with God for 40 days. That time offers the possibility of transforming your life and becoming a catalyst for God to do so much more in your life.

Over the last several years, I have purchased a handful of devotional books. With each one, I committed the time frame for which they were written. In those times with the Lord, He moved in my life. Each shifted my trajectory closer to where He wanted me. That's what gives me joy. That's what makes the effort worth it. And, 40 days is almost long enough to form a solid habit.

So, thank you for trusting me enough to choose *Invincible*, and thank you for allowing me to have a part in your daily devotional life.

I feel weird saying it out loud, or I guess in this case writing it, but this book began with a dream and a new album download.

As a result of God using a couple of those important devotional books to change my wife's life and my own life, we took a step of faith. We left a pastorate at a church where God was working and where there were people we loved dearly, to step out with no job, no home, and no security. Others have made bigger jumps, but it was a tough transition for us. In the process of making that move, I had a dream. You know, one of those dreams that you knew was not from something you ate before bedtime.

It felt like the Lord was speaking through it.

3

The setting of the dream was a post-apocalyptic world raging in war. It resembled a video game like Halo, or versions of Call of Duty. I was given a mission to retrieve something that was behind enemy lines. In the dream, I was afraid, but I pushed ahead. To my surprise, I was able to slip past the enemy without being detected. Gunfire whizzed by, never getting close to me. I made it deep behind enemy lines unnoticed, and then all the way back, unharmed and undetected. In the process, I even believed I couldn't be harmed or caught. It was as if I was invincible.

The dream was so vivid, I wrote it down the next morning. It stayed with me in this new step of faith. I'm still not exactly sure what the Lord was telling me through the dream, but I sensed He'd take care of me in this God-given adventure.

I mentioned invincibility earlier, but it wasn't until I downloaded the album, "Unleased," by the Christian rock band, Skillet, that God's message to me became clearer. That album was released at about the same time as my dream. Each song was devoted to being invincible in Christ. Skillet helped me articulate what I saw in the dream—that in following God's call, I was invincible. As I reflected, I was reminded of how God is invincible. Scripture shows that God made His people invincible in the missions He called them to, so perhaps I could be invincible in real life as well.

Such an idea, in our human logic, can be a hard pill to swallow. But we must take it. Why? Because each day our faith is challenged, and prophetically, those challenges will increase in number and intensity. We must find confidence knowing God is able and take bold steps that require courage and confidence in Him.

The pages ahead are simply stories from Scripture about God taking care of His people. All He did then, He can do again. My hope is for your confidence in God to be built up to the point where you trust Him for and in everything. Will you take the 40-day journey and strengthen your faith muscles?

I've been blessed to partner with Rita Halter Thomas on this devotional book. Rita has years of experience in journalism and writing in general. She's a writer. I'm more of an idea spreader. She touched every page of my first book, *Spiritual Prepper*, helping me secure an agent and a publishing contract. That worked so well, we thought we'd do it again. She's gracious to combine it all in one voice.

A Welcome from Rita

What an incredible honor it is to partner with Jake to bring you *Invincible*. Jake's education and years in pastoral ministry best position him to write this book. I simply work with the words he puts on paper to ensure they communicate what's on his heart.

Even in its developmental stage, *Invincible* touched my heart and stretched my faith muscles. I am eager to read it again, in its completed form, and to take the 40-day journey from start to finish as intended. I'm confident that if you allow God to work in your heart, your faith will be challenged, stretched, and strengthened.

Are you ready to add a little bulk to your faith muscles?

A Spiritual Prepper Resource

We call this devotional book a *Spiritual Prepper* resource. Hopefully, you've read my book, *Spiritual Prepper.* If not, I hope you choose to do so. In summary, it picks up the warning in Matthew 24:10, that many will turn away and warns that "anyone" could be any one of us. As of 2015, 42 million Americans have left the faith. We're not even in the prophetic time reference in this verse. We're not doing well at standing firm.

I wrote *Spiritual Prepper* to warn of this danger and call readers to spiritually prepare. Just as a doomsday prepper preps for physical danger, we should prepare for the spiritual battles that lie ahead. Instead of building bunkers, stocking up on food, and storing ammunition, we need to be growing closer to our Lord. We need to learn His Word in depth, increase our confidence in Him, and strengthen our faith muscles. We must do these things if we hope to spiritually survive the onslaught of attacks against our faith and our Lord.

Invincible, and the spiritual preparedness resources that follow it, are meant to be tools to help you prepare. One area of spiritual prepping is to build our confidence in God. That's what the 40-day journey of *Invincible* is meant to accomplish.

A Faith Sustaining Resource

There are many books out there that call us to step out in faith, take the plunge, and obey the Spirit, though the journey sounds crazy. They sound a call to trust God for the mission He's given us. I could list several that have done that very thing for my life. Many books have been written that call us to get out of the boat. They encourage us to launch new ministries, step into new roles, and make other radical moves in following God's call.

We need these types of books. However, resources that help us stay the course are in short supply. That's where *Invincible* comes in.

Taking the first step of faith is difficult, but many times the ones that follow are even more so. The fire that burns within us often burns greater at the beginning, fueling that initial step. The trick is keeping the fire sustained—fanning it and feeding it so the flame continues to burn.

It's one thing to face lions like those in Mark Batterson's *In a Pit with a Lion on a Snowy Day*, but it's another to stay in the pit when the lion starts to get the best of us.

It's one thing to chase a wild goose like how the Holy Spirit is described in another favorite of mine from Mark Batterson, *Wild Goose Chase*, but when the goose leads you through difficult terrain, it can be frightening.

It's one thing to follow Henry Blackaby's study, *Experiencing God,* and then go join God where He is working. It's another thing altogether to continue when "where God was working" drags on and on with what seems like no results.

Yes, staying the course in a calling is difficult. To respond to a shortage of resources to build up the faith needed for that course, we wrote *Invincible*.

Through this 40-day journey, we hope you find encouragement and develop habits to help sustain you as you walk out God's calling on your life.

The Plan

You'll find some personal anecdotes, but strangely, for a modern devotional book, it's short on extrabiblical illustrations. Rather, the biblical accounts of the feats of God are the illustrations. Each devotion is a story of how God took care of His people. We help the reader connect the account to present-day life. Each account is followed by a verse to offer invincible encouragement.

Many times, we use a focus verse from the Psalms. We also often use two scriptural references to show how Scripture interacts with Scripture.

The forty days are separated into six "one-week" segments. Each week focuses on a specific theme to reinforce the great feats of God as He cared for His people.

The weeks are:

Victory

Provision

Protection

Impossible

Beyond

In the End

Appendices are included that provide additional tools to help build your confidence in God.

Disclaimers

Before diving into the devotionals, we've two disclaimers to make. The first is—**WE'RE NOT INVINCIBLE APART FROM CHRIST**. We've purposefully tried to make statements that express that you're invincible and victorious. This didn't come easy for either of us because we know we're nothing apart from Christ in us. However, God is calling each one of us to take the steps of faith we need to make. We must make a move, and in that move, we're invincible. It's important to know how this applies to us personally, but we want you to understand: There is no way can we possess these traits outside of belonging to and following Jesus.

The second disclaimer is—**THESE PROMISES APPLY WHEN WE'RE FAITHFULLY FOLLOWING JESUS.** There are lots of resources that relay the promises of God to take care of us, but I often cringe because, though God has made that promise, we also have a responsibility to follow Him. In our culture, we want to live our lives and have God just bless us. However, His promises of invincibility, victory, provision, and protection are for when we're seeking Him, not when we're out in left field. Granted, God often takes care of us while we're off the path, but we must recognize that as His mercy and grace. He's not obligated to do so.

It's Time

Again, thank you for selecting *Invincible* and for making this forty-day commitment. We've worked hard to provide a tool to help build your confidence in God. It's important to us because so much is at stake. We pray that you will let the Lord speak through the accounts of His work in Scripture and encourage you. We pray you will know that, in Him, you're **INVINCIBLE.**

When God fights for His people, He brings them victory. Often, we look around, and it appears the world is out of control. It seems that evil is winning, and Christians are on the losing end. But that's not the reality. It's not the reality of God's people in the past, nor is it now. God will win. He's invincible. Since He is victorious, He will give His people victory. He will give you victory.

DAY 1
Victory in Every Valley

From 1 Samuel 17
The Account of God Giving David Victory Over Goliath

The Challenge

In 1 Samuel 17, we find one of the most retold Bible stories—David versus Goliath. David was sent by his father to get a report and take food to his brothers, who were camped with Saul's army at the Valley of Elah. The Israelites had been in position on one hill for 40 days, while the Philistines held the opposite ridge. Goliath, a literal giant and *the* champion warrior of the Philistines, was terrorizing the Israelites twice a day. Each day, he'd step out into the valley, mock the God of Israel, and challenge an Israelite to fight him. The Israelites remained frozen in fear.

Knowing the outcome of this story, their fear seems foolish. They were battle-hardened soldiers. Tough men. Valiant men who lived in a trying time in history. Their fear shows that Goliath must've been terrifying.

Again, because we know the outcome, we often overlook just how daunting Goliath would've been with his size, ability, experience, and the lore attached to him.

He stood 9'6" tall, twice the height of the average man of that time. He weighed an estimated 450–530 pounds. His armor weighed as much as David. The head of his spear was 17 pounds, which outweighed spearheads of that day by 16 pounds. The spearheads of that time were typically eight inches long. Goliath's spear is estimated to have been 26 inches long, making the length of his entire spear far longer than any spear the Israelites would have had.

Daunting to say the least.

We may never face a literal giant, but we do encounter giant obstacles and enemies of the calling of God on our lives. Like the Israelite soldiers, we might even be justified to take cover. But when David arrived at the edge of the valley and heard Goliath's challenge and defiance of Yahweh, he voiced a desire to face the giant.

Why would he?

He recognized some things greater than a giant in the valley at work—the nature and promises of His God, the calling upon Israel, and the calling upon himself.

David's persistence took him down into the valley armed with only a sling and five stones. In striking contrast, Goliath towered over David. The Philistine was protected by full armor and shield and was armed with a huge sword and spear. It was a snapshot for the ages—a picture that would motivate Israel for years to come and still motivates us today; a young boy with a sling in front of the giant.

David didn't march out onto that plain for a personal victory or accomplishment. He marched out to fight for the Lord's honor. He marched out according to the Lord's instruction.

Granted, we see no place in this narrative of God speaking to David, calling him to take on this task. However, there were plenty of existing orders from the Lord which David obeyed.

Israel had been called to conquer the land. They'd been instructed to wipe out the Philistines. For years, they'd been repeatedly taught to trust the Lord and let Him fight for them.

David, already anointed as the next King of Israel, carried the confidence of that hidden detail into the fight. Knowing God's plan for his life, David trusted that no measly giant would prevent it—David was invincible through the invincibility of God. A defeat by Goliath would've made God a liar.

At the time of David's life, the testimony of Abraham, Jacob, Joseph, Moses, Joshua, and the Judges stood before him. He knew the promises God had made to Israel and the impossible victories God had already given.

The Victory

The giant that terrified an entire army fell with one stone slung from David. God had given a victory for the ages. David stood unharmed.

David took God at His Word. Unphased by Goliath, he marched onto the plain, convinced God would give him the victory. And the Lord did. God made him invincible. David wasn't surprised.

Later in life, while possibly even looking back at the victory in the Valley of Elah, he wrote: ***Even though I walk through the darkest valley, I will fear no evil, for You are with me; Your rod and Your staff, they comfort me (Psalm 23:4, NIV).***

Before David walked into the literal dark valley to fight Goliath, King Saul warned him of the danger. But David responded, citing how God had given past victories over a lion and bear. Knowing the Lord had been with him then, David knew God would still be with him when he faced the giant.

By the time David wrote Psalm 23, he'd witnessed a string of God-given victories. He knew God would see him through even the darkest of valleys.

Psalm 23:4 is often used on sympathy cards, but it's much more than words to comfort the grieving. It's a battle cry. If you follow the Lord into any valley, regardless of how dark, you can trust that He will bring you out the victor—even if a literal giant is waiting for you.

Today's Faith Builder

Like David recounted to King Saul, reflect on the victories God has already given you.

DAY 2
Victory Belongs to Yahweh

From Exodus 1–14
The Account of God Rescuing Israel from Egypt

The Challenge

Hindsight allows us to see the opportunities we missed. Looking back, it's easier to see our ability to accomplish more if we'd realized our own potential. Unfortunately, in the moment, we can't see the reality of the opportunity or our abilities.

Have you ever looked back at your life and seen a missed opportunity, or how you could have accomplished more if you'd known your true potential? Or have you ever watched someone fall short because they didn't live up to their potential? It's frustrating to see and experience. We're especially susceptible to this when we're focused on the enemy rather than considering our own God-given potential.

We aren't the only ones.

In Exodus 1:6–11, we see the Israelites in that situation. Over the years of captivity in Egypt, they increased enough in number to become a real threat to Egypt. Pharaoh grew nervous, knowing that if they ever recognized their potential, the Israelites could inflict great harm. He realized that if they decided to turn against the him or join with another army, they could possibly defeat him.

But Israel *didn't* see their potential, and they certainly didn't know the potential of their God. Once Pharaoh recognized the threat Israel could become, he doubled-down on his cruelty toward them. He not only enslaved them deeper and became stricter, but he also ordered their newborns to be killed. It appears that Israel didn't realize their population had grown to be comparable to that of the Egyptians.

What they *did* know was that Egypt was one of the most powerful kingdoms on Earth.

Their army was second to none. They'd been victorious over and over again.

Perhaps the Israelites credited the Egyptian gods for those repeated victories. Perhaps they began to consider the possibility that the Egyptian gods were greater than their God— the God of Abraham, Isaac, and Jacob.

In our readings in the Old Testament, we often condemn ancient Israel for how quickly they turned against God and especially how they grumbled during the Exodus. However, we should keep in mind that, at that point in history, they really hadn't received many promises from God or witnessed Him do miraculous feats prior to the Exodus. In later times, God would tell Israel to look back at the Exodus and the parting of the Red Sea, but this was the moment in which that milestone was about to happen. At that point in history, the Israelites' knowledge of God hinged on what had been passed down to them about Abraham, Isaac, and Jacob. They knew God had promised to make them a mighty nation and to give them a particular land.

They knew God had given Abraham and Sarah their son, Isaac, against all odds. They also should've known that God was the Creator.

In reality, they had a small sampling of God's work. It's amazing that they remained faithful to Him for those many years in Egypt.

Now, they *could* have looked around and noticed how God had grown them into a mighty nation, but again, they didn't see their own potential in God.

So, here was a people who'd been promised to be a mighty nation and possess a Promised Land. They were the unique people of the one true God, but they were enslaved. Every day, the burden grew harder. There was no way out. The Egyptians seemed impossible to defeat or even challenge. Things appeared hopeless until the people of Israel cried out to God.

The Victory

Their cry is recorded in Exodus 3:7–9. There, we read that God heard them and responded. And wow, did He respond! Exodus 3:7b–8a says, "I have heard them crying out because of their slave drivers, and I am concerned about their suffering. So, I have come down to rescue them from the hand of the Egyptians and to bring them up out of that land into a good and spacious land, a land flowing with milk and honey."

That phrase, "He came down," is so powerful. God moved. He sent Moses and then caused numerous plagues to afflict the Egyptians. These plagues weren't only miraculous feats, but also challenges against the Egyptian gods. When

Pharaoh refused to relent, God sent the plague of death to the firstborns. In Goshen, the Hebrews covered their doorposts with the blood of the lamb and all their firstborns were spared, but none of the Egyptian firstborns survived.

Finally, Pharaoh, the most powerful man on Earth, relented. He bowed to the command of the God of his slaves. Not only were the Hebrews allowed to leave, but the Egyptians brought them plunder. Their journey was financed by the same people who wouldn't let them go.

God won. Big time. He proved Himself to be the God above all.

Five hundred years later, reflecting on the victories He had received, David wrote: **He [God] rescued me from my powerful enemy, from my foes, who were too strong for me (Psalm 18:17, NIV).**

This was true for David, and it was certainly true for all of Israel at the Exodus. It's true for us today.

Today's Faith Builder:

Like David remembered, and Israel saw in Egypt, remember God gives victory when the foes are stronger than us. Consider your foes—do you believe God can beat them?

DAY 3
Victory Over the Fortified

From Joshua 5–6
The Account of God Giving Israel Victory Over Jericho

The Challenge

Oh, how their hearts must have melted at the sight of Jericho. After 40 years of wilderness wanderings, Israel passed deeper into the Transjordan plain than they had when they rebelled four decades before. This time, they were moving forward to do what their forefathers hadn't done. They were ready to enjoy their promised land. They prepared themselves and then crossed over the Jordan. God had told them this land was their land. They were promised victory, but once they crossed the river, what did they see—a towering double-walled impregnable city. That's what was waiting for them.

In the 1950s, archaeological work by Kathleen Kenyon found that the city was surrounded by a large earthen embankment with double walls. In all, there were three walls. A retaining wall that held in the inclining embankment, a tall outside wall that rose from atop the retaining wall, and then an inner wall. First, the retaining wall stood 12–15 feet high. On top of that, was the rest of the outside wall. It was six feet wide and rose to 20–26 feet high. Then, on top of the embankment mound, was the inner wall, which was also six feet wide. The distance from the ground to the top of the second inner wall was estimated to be about 46 feet.

Impregnable is correct.

Impossible would probably be fitting.

Imagine their deflated hope. This huge obstacle stood between the Israelites at the start of their mission to conquer the Promised Land.

Have you felt like that in your life, or especially in your calling? God sends you out, and you're all gung-ho, only to run into a wall—a wall impossible to scale.

The Israelites' response at the sight of this incredible fortified city isn't revealed in this account in Joshua. We do know that, 40 years prior, 10 of the first 12 spies into the city said, as recorded in Numbers 13:28 and 31, "The people who live there are powerful, and the cities are fortified and very large. We can't attack those people; they are stronger than we are." That report crushed the Israelites, and they aborted the mission.

This time, Israel didn't rebel. Somehow, Joshua kept them moving forward.

On top of all the promises God made to His people and to Joshua, an angel identified as the "Commander of the Army of the Lord" appeared to Joshua. The Lord said, "I have delivered Jericho into your hands."

With that promise and the bizarre instructions that the Lord gave, Joshua and the Israelites marched on to Jericho.

The Victory

There is no way Israel could have scaled the walls of Jericho. They had no chance of conquering the city, yet, they'd been promised victory.

The Lord had given Joshua a wild strategy: march around the city once for six days, then on the seventh day, march seven times with the priests blowing the trumpets. Then, the walls would fall.

They marched by faith.

They blew the trumpets as instructed.

And the walls came crumbling down.

Jericho had been defeated.

God had broken through the most difficult of defenses.

In Psalm 18, we find David, the author of the psalm, reflecting over his life and the victories God gave him. David, in his life of war and conquests, faced cities greatly fortified, however, none as much as Joshua found at Jericho. Somewhere between the remembrance of Jericho and his own experience, David wrote: **With your help I can advance against a troop; with my God I can scale a wall (Psalm 18:29, NIV).**

In your following of Christ, and in obedience to His instruction, you may come up against a proverbial Jericho. As you look at the task ahead, it seems impenetrable. It seems impossible to scale. Often, such a challenge comes at the outset, as it did for the Israelites. At first, they shrunk back and spent 40 years in the desert. After, they marched on until they stood in its fearsome shadow. Then and only then, did God tell them "how" to conquer it—and even that didn't make sense. They had to trust God.

They had to trust that their God could scale a wall.

Today's Faith Builder:

What is the fortified wall before you? Whatever it is, keep marching. Instruction will come. Trust and obey.

DAY 4
Victory with Any Weapon

From Judges 15
The Account of God Giving Samson Victory Over a Thousand

The Challenge

For those seeking to follow the Lord faithfully or carry out a calling in this age (especially in America), limited resources are too often one of the most frustrating challenges. This is especially true for new ministries and new ventures breaking beyond the status quo.

Have you been there—thinking if only you had this or that, then you'd be able to carry out the venture? Or maybe you're following God's direction for your life—you know you're where you need to be, but you're not sure how you're going to financially survive.

Too often, God's people seem to face this scenario.

One of the most remarkable victories told in Scripture was accomplished with a surprising resource.

Samson was blessed with incredible supernatural strength, like a comic book hero of today. But that notorious strength was a God-given provision for his calling—to deliver his people from the Philistines.

Bad choices and a series of unfortunate events led Samson to finally rise to his calling. In vengeance for the giving away of his Philistine wife, he caught 300 foxes and tied their tails together with a lighted torch. He released them on the Philistines' fields, vineyards, and olive trees, decimating their food and economy, naturally drawing anger from them. In addition to destroying their crops and vineyards, Samson attacked and slaughtered many of them, further fueling their anger.

Unable to find him, the Philistines threatened the Israelites, leading Samson's own people to bind him in strong ropes and turn him over to his enemy. Let this fact sink in: It took 3,000 men to bind him. THREE T H O U S A N D.

So, the promised deliverer of Israel is bound and left in the wilderness, unarmed, and eventually surrounded by at least 1,000 well-armed Philistine soldiers.

Samson had a calling. He had a mission, yet, he barely had begun to scratch the surface of all God called him to do. Surely, the Lord wouldn't let His champion end like this. What about what God had promised to do through Samson? Samson was meant to be a deliverer of Israel. God had given him his strength for that purpose.

In this moment, what was he to do?

He was:

Surrounded by his enemy.

Outnumbered at least a thousand to one.

No one coming to his rescue.

Bound.

No weapon.

But Samson did have a history before him of God's called men and women winning against all odds. Through Gideon and his 300 men, God defeated thousands more. God had empowered Shamgar to defeat 600 Philistines with an ox goad. Let's not forget the victory against the giants in Canaan during the time of Joshua. God accomplished the impossible by bringing down the walls of Jericho and parting the Red Sea.

To be fair in those instances, the heroes of faith had been prepared before the fight with a strategy and instruction from God. Samson didn't have that.

Samson also might've had more confidence at that moment if he hadn't been literally strapped, or if he had the resources of his enemy.

The Victory

As the Philistines closed in, God supernaturally gave even more strength to the strong man. God allowed the restrictions around Samson to fall, and then he found the jawbone of a donkey. Not with a sword, spear, or even a machine gun (something that might be more ideal in a situation like that), but with a jawbone and the strength of the Lord, Samson slew 1,000 Philistines. Marvel's Avengers-type stuff. It's incredible what God allowed one man to do with a jawbone.

The psalmist, David, was a warrior who often found himself on the run and in less than ideal situations—even while still walking in obedience to the Lord. Recounting how God had provided in those moments, and later as king of a prospering nation that God had supplied, he wrote: **You armed me with**

strength for battle; You humbled my adversaries before me (Psalm 18:39, NIV).

It sounds as if David took the words right out of Samson's mouth with that verse. They both had the same experience because God comes through. He's going to give victory; therefore, He'll provide what we need. It may come in dramatic fashion. It may seem as inefficient as a jawbone when we think we need a machine gun. But the tools for victory will come.

Today's Faith Builder:

What do you think you're lacking? Maybe the enemies of your walk with the Lord or of your calling (see Appendix 2 for help on discovering your calling) are pressing down on you. Perhaps you believe victory would be easier if certain resources were available to you. Or maybe you feel strapped, restrained in some way. Let me encourage you to put those thoughts aside and trust that God has or will give you all you need for victory.

DAY 5
Victory through Prayer

From 2 Chronicles 32, Isaiah 36–38
The Account of God Giving Hezekiah Victory Over the Assyrians

The Challenge

Though you follow the One True God, the Victor, whose plans won't be thwarted, life conditions or challenges in obeying your call may appear hopeless. This was the case of the Israelite army. They believed no one among them would ever match up to the power of Goliath. They believed they might remain in Egyptian captivity forever. Often, the path of obedience rounds a corner and collides with bleakness. You may even suffer great loss.

King Hezekiah and the nation of Judah found themselves in one of the most hopeless situations any person of God has perhaps been found. They suffered tremendous loss and were pushed to the max.

For decades, God raised up prophets to warn the ten tribes of northern Israel (headquartered in Samaria) and Judah in the south (headquartered in Jerusalem) to turn from their idolatry and turn back to God. And if they did not, God would bring judgment, and they would be carried out of the land. In the North, no king listened. In the South, few did like King Hezekiah.

29

Eventually, in 722 B.C., it happened. Assyria marched into Israel and exiled the ten tribes of the North. Isaiah, prophesying at that time, warned Judah that if they were not faithful to God, they could be next.

Within twenty years, the Assyrian king, Sennacherib, brought his army into Judah. The Assyrian army was considered the cruelest and most ruthless force the world had ever seen to date. In this Judean campaign, 46 cities were destroyed, and it's believed that 200,000 citizens of Judah were exiled. These were all the major cities of the nation. Finally, they seized the second most important city, Lachish.

After overtaking all the cities in Judah, Sennacherib's 185,000 soldiers marched on Jerusalem and besieged the city. Inside the city, the surviving people of Judah were pinned in on every side. Hezekiah had made preparations to defend his people and help them survive the siege, but against 185,000 soldiers and with no one to come to his aid, the situation was hopeless.

Charged by God to protect His people, Hezekiah appeared to be heading towards failure.

As the siege continued, and the hearts of Jerusalem continued to drain of all hope, Sennacherib sent a letter to the people of Judah insulting God and telling them Hezekiah would fail them.

The Victory

Hezekiah lost all the cities in his kingdom. An insurmountable force surrounded the final stronghold. His efforts to save them proved futile and his people lost hope.

Hezekiah sought counsel from his trusted advisor, Isaiah, who reassured him not to be afraid, that God would provide a supernatural rescue.

Still, the evidence did not seem to make that report trustworthy. With nowhere to turn, Hezekiah took the letter from Sennacherib into the temple and spread it out before the Lord. At the end of his rope, he asked the Lord to take care of it.

And as God does, He took care of it.

King Hezekiah awoke the next morning to find 185,000 corpses around the city.

An angel had been sent to wipe out the threat, to wipe out hopelessness.

God will always be the victor. Though His people and His cause may seem hopelessly under siege, He will win.

He wasn't surrounded by 185,000 soldiers, but King David was on the run from his son, Absalom and his army, and had appeared to have met his end when he wrote these words: **I will not fear though tens of thousands assail me on every side (Psalm 3:6, NIV).**

At some point in your life, if you have not already, you will find yourself surrounded. There may come a time of hopelessness. Survival may appear bleak, though probably never to the extent Hezekiah faced. He tried hard to save his people himself. He built a tunnel to a spring to give access to water. (His tunnel can be seen today.) He built up an army and trained them. He built shields and weapons and refortified the city. He pursued alliances. All in vain.

King Hezekiah prayed one night, and more than He ever thought could be accomplished was accomplished.

Today's Faith Builder:

Whatever challenge you face—pray. Maybe write it down, and just as Hezekiah spread the letter before the Lord, lay your troubles before Him.

DAY 6
Victory Over Our Only True Enemy

From John 19–20
The Account of Jesus' Resurrection

The Challenge

Invincible.

As a follower of Jesus, if we're honest with ourselves, believing we're invincible seems a bit sketchy. Sure, deep within our spirit, a country-church-mid-sermon amen sits ready on our tongues. There's an illumination within our hearts that knows it's a true statement, but what we see as reality casts a shadow of doubt. Our minds overrule the truth in our hearts because we see Christians persecuted, marginalized, beaten, imprisoned, and killed all throughout history.

We also recognize that we live in a time when Christians are persecuted more now than any other time in history. We know, apart from only one generation of believers, we'll all die. Our churches are empty and closing at record rates in America. Most likely you bought this devotional book online because there's hardly a Christian bookstore left on Earth. We're ridiculed and attacked in the media. The list could go on.

We suffer from sickness—some common, some catastrophic. We experience pain in relationships—even church relationships. These include everything from betrayal to loss. We've been broken, or at some point, we will be. Frankly, we have no idea of the difficulty we'll face tomorrow or even in the next hour.

Bottom line: we suffer and will most likely die—all of which seems anything but invincible.

Physical death seems to be the biggest obstacle in believing we're invincible. However, the biblical reality is that death for a believer is a blessing. It's a step up. It's beneficial because Heaven awaits. Immortality and true invincibility await that last breath.

Therefore, when the very worst happens to us and we die physically—we benefit.

That sounds pretty invincible to me, how about you?

How do we know that's true?

It's been done.

The One who claimed to be the promised Messiah of the Old Testament, Jesus, revealed Himself on Earth. After three years of displaying His power on Earth, proving He was the invincible God who would make His people invincible, He was arrested. Falsely accused. Beaten severely. Mocked. Sentenced to die by crucifixion.

Though many discounted His claim to be the long-awaited Messiah, some believed. Those followers watched Him face the phony trial. They watched as He carried His own cross through Jerusalem. They watched as He carried that cross up the hill called Golgotha. They watched as His hands were spread out on the crossbeam and nailed down. With their own eyes, they saw the nails pierce through both feet. They witnessed Roman soldiers raise the cross and drop it into place, dislocating most of their Messiah's joints. They saw Him fight for breath as fluid filled his lungs. They heard Him scream out in anguish. They also heard Him say it was finished. They heard His last breath. They also saw the Roman guard drive the spear into Jesus' side causing blood and water to spill out. They heard Him pronounced dead. They saw Him lowered from the cross and carried away to be prepared for burial. They knew He was laid in a tomb, and the large stone door was rolled in place. They saw the Roman seal on the stone and the Roman guards around the tomb.

The One who claimed to be invincible was dead.

The One who said He could make them invincible wasn't even able to save Himself.

The One who claimed to be the Victor was terribly defeated.

Can you imagine being a follower of Jesus at that time? They had believed and devoted their lives to Him, but He died.

The Victory

On the first day of the week, three days after Jesus' death, Mary Magdalene and a group of other believing women went to the tomb. There, they found the stone rolled away, the tomb empty, and the body of Jesus gone.

Surprised and perplexed, they eventually saw two angels who pronounced the news—He'd risen! He had beaten death.

Soon, Jesus appeared before them in a brilliant glorified body.

He was invincible.

He was the Victor over death.

The Bible calls Jesus the first fruit of this resurrection—His invincible followers will do the same.

With this resurrection, Jesus proved He had started and would finish what Isaiah had spoken: **He will swallow up death forever; and the Lord God will wipe away tears from all faces, and the reproach of His people He will take away from all the earth, for the Lord has spoken (Isaiah 25:8, ESV).**

This victory that we have through Jesus over our one true enemy, death, is what led Paul to write the words, "O, Death where is your sting?"

Today's Faith Builder:

Not even the worst you may face—death—will defeat you. Consider that you are invincible and victorious in Christ.

DAY 7
Victory is Yours

From Matthew 28:20
The Account of Your Life in Christ

The Challenge

The story of God and His people didn't end with the Bible. The book of Acts didn't end when Paul died in Rome. I'm not saying words should be added to the Bible, but I'm saying the God who performed miracles for and through His people in Scripture still performs miracles. The God who called people to follow Him, gave them particular missions or tasks, and gave them victory in that calling, still does those things. God is the same; He hasn't changed. He still has His people—that's you. He still has callings and missions—that's what He's given you. He still gives victory, too.

The book of Joshua tells the story of Joshua following God's call in leading the people to conquer the Promised Land. The book of Esther tells of Esther's bravery to risk her life to save her people. Your life is such a book. It's true for us, the authors of *Invincible*. There's a proverbial book of Jake and book of Rita. Our obedience to write *Invincible* is only a chapter or two in it. There's a book for God's work through you—The book of _____ (your name here).

Like the book of Judges, the book of Jake and the book of Rita contain failures, but there are also victories—and there will be more. God didn't call us just to let the giant slay us, the Egyptians to keep us in bondage, the walls of Jericho to stop us, the 185,000 to destroy us, or even death to defeat us. We're victorious as long as we stay on the path God is leading. The same is true for you.

But like all the victories gained by the heroes of faith we read in Scripture and history, challenges stand before you, before us. It probably doesn't take much for you to remember them. Surely, they are at the forefront of your mind.

You may be hiding behind the rocks, afraid to enter the valley. You may stand like the Israelites in Egypt, unable to see God's potential in yourself. You may be like the Israelites discouraged by impossible walls to climb. You may be hopeless like Hezekiah. You may even be facing your own death or the death of someone you love. But just as God stepped in and gave victory, He will for you.

Though you may be in bondage to sin or guilt from the past.

Though you may be lonely.

Though you may have failed.

Though you may be hurt emotionally.

Though the calling isn't working out.

Though the ministry appears to be failing.

Though you are broke, and the bills keep mounting.

Though you're sick.

Whatever it is—you're invincible because the mission is not your mission, it's God's mission. He called you.

You may need to face your fears like David, cry out like the Israelites in Egypt, follow God's crazy plan like the Israelites at Jericho, lay it before the Lord like Hezekiah, or just trust God's promises will come to pass. Whatever it is, do it. Move forward.

The Victory

How do I know God will give you victory?

Well, personally, I'm still learning.

I know that before Jesus ascended to Heaven, He gave His followers, including us, an overarching mission. Today, whatever your instruction and calling may be, it falls under that mission. He told them and us to make disciples of the world.

Starting with 12 disciples, they had an insane uphill battle.

History books prove they did it. They turned the world upside down.

Though persecuted and facing challenge after challenge, they were victorious.

Just like we will be.

They were victorious because Jesus made this promise: **Surely, I am with you always, to the very end of the age (Matthew 28:20, NIV).**

For two thousand years, He has kept that promise, and He will keep it with you.

Today's Faith Builder:

Settle in your heart that just as His people have been victorious in the past, you also will be victorious.

Week 2

PROVISION

When God sent His people anywhere or called them to do anything, He provided. When we're in the midst of following God, and carrying out the mission He's called us to, it can get tough. We often don't know how we'll accomplish it. How will we meet the needs we have, or acquire what is needed to accomplish what He's called us to do? Often, it looks as if we're going to be in over our heads to fulfill our task or calling, but God shows up every time. He did it all throughout the Bible, all throughout history, and He still comes through even now. He's fully capable. God will provide for His people, including you.

DAY 8
Provision for All Our Needs

From 1 Kings 17
The Account of God Providing All Elijah Needed to Survive

The Challenge

"Father, if I do what you're asking, how will I survive?"

"Father, if I take this step, I'm not going to have what I need."

"Father, after hearing this news, I have no idea how I'm going to make it."

Have you asked God similar questions?

Have you ever gotten a health report, yours or someone else's, that left you wondering how you or they would survive? Maybe you received a bill or checked a bank statement and wondered if you'd reach the end of the money before you reached the end of the month. Perhaps you've been led by the Holy Spirit to step out in faith, completely uncertain of how you'd feed your family or even feed yourself. Or maybe you knew you needed to take a stand, knowing it might cost you your job and financial security.

If you haven't faced such a fork in the road of faith—keep following God and you will.

43

Every step of faith and every faithful life recorded in the Bible involves such a crisis.

And in each biblical account, God proved to be faithful, taking care of His people. He provided what they needed.

One of the most iconic examples of God's faithfulness found in Scripture is in the life of Elijah.

During the time of the divided kingdom, the northern ten tribes were already deep in idolatry when Ahab became their king. In 1 Kings 16:30-31 we read, "Ahab...did more evil in the eyes of the Lord than any of those [kings] before him...he also married Jezebel."

In a nation departed from God and deep in idol worship, Ahab indulged further than any other—so much so, his wife, Jezebel, became synonymous with evil.

In response to that sin, God sent His prophet Elijah to King Ahab with a loaded message. God called Elijah to pronounce the coming of an indefinite drought causing famine and other travesties. God granted Elijah authority over rain in some way, allowing rain to come only when Elijah spoke.

This bold move made Elijah a wanted man. Ahab wanted Elijah to make it rain and then kill him. Elijah, unsure of his own survival, obeyed God and made the bold pronouncement.

Like those who faithfully follow the Lord and trust Him, Elijah trusted God to take of him, but he had no idea how God would do it or to what extent.

The Provision

God provided Elijah with detailed instruction. God instructed him to hide in the Kerith Ravine where a brook there would supply water and ravens would feed him. Yes, ravens.

Elijah went.

Sure enough, there was a brook that supplied water.

Sure enough, he was well hidden. Ahab's men did not find him in the three years Elijah was hidden.

And believe it or not, ravens brought him bread and meat every morning and every evening. This continued for some time until the brook dried up, and God provided another place of provision in Zarephath of Sidon. There, God used a widow to provide Elijah with food and drink in another miraculous way.

God gave Elijah a mission. Elijah took a step of faith with uncertainty before him. He obeyed. Then, God did what He always does. He came through. He provided. I wonder if Elijah laughed when the ravens brought him food? I wonder if he remembered how God provided the Israelites with manna and quail in the wilderness? Whatever his thoughts, he learned what the psalmist meant when he wrote: **The lions may grow weak and hungry, but those who seek the Lord lack no good thing (Psalm 34:10, NIV).**

Yes, Elijah was a remarkable man of God, but God's provision is not limited to only him. It may not be ravens that feed you, but God surely will provide all you need.

Today's Faith Builder:

God provides. He just does. Set your heart and mind to the fact that no matter what you face or are called to do, God will provide all you need.

DAY 8
Provision of the "How"

From Genesis 6–9
The Account of God Providing the Animals for the Ark

The Challenge

How's that going to work?

Can you imagine the number of times God's been asked that question by those He's called and given a particular task or mission? Or from those facing a difficult trial, and He reassures their Spirit that's it going to be ok?

Chances are, you've asked that question, and if not, you will. Just simply living for God in this life is so countercultural that some things God leads us to do are head-scratchers. When God calls us to do certain things, He often leaves out the details. We're told the *what*, but not the *how*, which makes taking the obedient step of faith difficult. We're left asking: How's this going to work?

Consider Noah. Before the first rain ever fell on Earth, God called him to build an ark (ship). God planned to flood the earth. The ark would house at least two (in some cases seven) of every creature—animals, birds, reptiles, and insects—anything that would not survive in water for the duration of the rain and flood. Noah needed to gather and load any creature that would need land to survive.

Over 4,000 years later, despite all the scientific discoveries since, scientists still haven't figured out all the different kinds of animals that were aboard the ark.

Picture Noah working in our modern-day context minus the power tools. Imagine Noah building this large ark out in the front yard with all his neighbors passing by every day. His big boat project becoming the town spectacle with all the gossip. People coming by, mocking and scoffing as they ask, "Noah, what are you up to?"

Can you imagine him having to explain this massive, illogical project to his wife? And to his sons, with his daughters-in-law thinking he's crazy?

Beyond the concept of flooding, before rain ever fell from the sky, beyond the ridicule of people around him, beyond building this massive boat to heavenly specs—Noah would have to explain the whole animal thing.

Can you imagine what he thought?

Noah had to be asking, "How am I going to catch these animals? Where am I going to find them?"

He probably thought, "God said he'd bring them all here, but how's He going to do that? How's this going to work? And even if they make it here, how am I going to take care of them?"

The Provision

At some point near the completion or after the completion of the ark, out of nowhere, likely in a bizarre but orderly fashion, male and female they came. Two by two, animals, birds, reptiles, bugs, and all other sorts of creatures came marching in toward Noah and onto the ark.

All that God said would happen was happening.

Noah and his family were finally seeing God's plan take shape, and His words take on flesh—and fur.

Eventually, in His divine time, everything God said came to pass. Because Noah and his family obeyed, they were saved. The mission was accomplished. They'd been obedient.

For perspective, you must realize that Noah had little precedent of God being faithful to His Word—at least we don't see much recorded in Scripture. The list of those who faithfully followed God up to that point had been scarce.

Once the animals came, and the door was shut, the rains fell. The water rose, the earth flooded, and Noah's family lived safely in the ark. Any doubts about the craziness of the ark project disappeared.

The animals supernaturally gathering to Noah may have been the first sign of God truly doing what He said.

I don't know exactly what God's calling is on your life, or what challenges you face. What I do know is that a lot of things He has called us to do are given to us in His Word. I can't tell you the number of times I've been left scratching my head.

How's this going to work?

What am I going to have to do? Sometimes I'm thinking, "This doesn't seem to be coming together."

The animals arriving two by two reminded Noah, and so they should remind us. God is going to come through. When life puts us in a tricky spot, or the task the Lord places before us seems undoable, let's remember what the psalmist noted: **My eyes are ever on the LORD, for only He will release my feet from the snare (Psalm 25:15, NIV).**

Today's Faith Builder:

Think about the details in your life that are tripping you up or causing you to stumble in your calling. List them. Get them all down on paper and then trust the Lord. He's got them.

DAY 10
Provision of Directions

From Exodus 14–Joshua 1
The Account of God Leading the Israelites in the Wilderness

The Challenge

As with Noah and his concerns regarding how to gather and load at least two of every kind of animal on the ark, he [we] surely thought [think], "How is this going to happen?" And, as with Noah, God often doesn't provide all the details.

Typically, when God calls His people to something, He gives them a vision of the final goal, but not the detailed steps to get there. The first step may be clear, but that's often it. Maybe you're like me. I like to know about a step-by-step plan. I want an overview. I want the big picture. I want to know exactly where I'm going.

I have a love-hate relationship with my GPS. I'm thankful for it, but I hate that it gives me just one step at a time. I want to see the whole route.

God often works like a GPS. Only after we take one step will He give us the next.

There may be no greater display of this than in the Exodus where God calls His people to Him into the Promised

51

Land. He wants them to leave Egypt and go to the land flowing with milk and honey. But, but, but...

There were so many unanswered questions. How will they know where to go? How will they stay in step with God? How was this going to work?

Sound familiar?

Likely over a million, even possibly two million Israelites found themselves in unfamiliar territory, with only a call to go to this land.

How would they know where to go?

The Provision

Early in the Exodus, God revealed His plan to guide His people. God would lead them with a pillar of cloud by day, and a pillar of fire by night. God provided a visual guide to lead the Israelites. If the cloud moved, they moved. If the pillar of fire moved, they moved. When the pillar of cloud or pillar fire rested, they rested.

By following this visible guide, they remained in step with the Lord, keeping them exactly where He wanted them to be.

Itinerary not included. The Israelites didn't know in advance when the cloud or pillar of fire would move or rest. They didn't know which direction it would take. But if they followed that guide, they would be OK. They would be right where God wanted them.

Although not always in the same big-billboard way God led Israel in the wilderness, He has always guided and continues to guide His people. The psalmist, David, found himself many times on the run—in the wilderness, in danger, or receiving a call from the Lord for particular campaigns.

Reflecting on that, he wrote in Psalm 31: **Since You are my rock and my fortress, for the sake of Your Name lead and guide me. Keep me free from the trap that is set for me, for You are my refuge (Psalm 31:3-4, NIV).**

God used many different ways to guide David. Whether through prophets, angelic messengers, or God's Spirit revealing direction, God gave David the steps to take. Throughout history, God has faithfully guided and instructed His people. He still does today.

The pillar of fire and the pillar of cloud were both very real, but they both are also symbolic to believers today. Our personal salvation and the continual walk with the Lord are pictured in the Exodus account. Just as the Israelites were in bondage in Egypt, we were in bondage in sin. Just as God sent Moses to be the deliverer, Jesus came as our Savior, to deliver us. God calls us to follow Him, eventually leading us into the ultimate Promised Land.

And, as with the Israelites in the wilderness, we're not alone. We're not left to figure out the journey on our own. We're not left to figure out whatever calling we have or the details of how to complete the task. We're not alone because we're given the Holy Spirit (see Appendix 2 for help on discovering your calling).

The Holy Spirit is within every believer giving us the directions we need. He's our guide.

Today's Faith Builder:

Ephesians 5:18 says, "Don't be drunk with wine, but be filled with the Holy Spirit." We tend to use that as a warning against drunkenness (which it is). However, it says much more than that. This verse is a direction on how to be guided by the Holy Spirit. Being filled with the Holy Spirit means that if we give Him reign in our lives, He will influence us—in the right way, for the right purpose.

Are you ready to move out of the way and let Him influence you?

DAY 11
Provision of the Necessities

From Exodus 14–Joshua 1
The Account of God Providing Food and Drink for the Israelites in the Wilderness

The Challenge

"The devil is in the details."

Chances are, you've heard that saying. Chances also are, at some point, you've experienced avoidable problems if only some important details hadn't been left out. How do you feel moving ahead when someone fails to provide necessary details?

As mentioned in the previous two devotions, when seeking God and following Him by faith, God usually leaves out the details. And boy, do we ever worry over those details.

Taking blind steps with little explanation often makes following difficult. The mission becomes harder because we think we need to know everything about the mission.

God often withholds the details, leaving us to follow by faith.

The Israelites experienced this in the wilderness.

Think about the scene of the Exodus. We're told in Scripture there were over 600,000 men of fighting age, and scholars believe the Israelite population to have been as high as two million people. Those who oppose that number do so, not because of the scriptural text, but because of the sheer impossibility of the situation.

Not only was there a ridiculous amount of people, but they all wandered a desolate, uninhabited land prior to reaching the land promised to them by God.

We read how the Lord used a pillar of fire and a pillar of smoke to guide their steps. He directed the steps to take, when to go, and when to wait. But what about other important details imperative to their survival? Water and food for two million people is an unquestionable core necessity.

How would they be sustained?

When we allow ourselves to become distracted by the details, following the Lord can be inhibited. Often, and especially initially, when God calls us to take a step of faith, we focus on what is lacking: resources, funds, education, training, etc.

We wonder as we try to figure it all out: How will we survive? How's this going to work?

You're probably picking up on the fact that when God calls you to something, not only does He give you victory, He provides for the victory.

I see myself in the Israelites as they grumbled and moaned—even as God provided for them day by day. Maybe you do as well. But do we really believe God would have rescued His people out of Egypt just to send them into the wilderness to die?

Would they die of thirst?

Would they starve?

Will you?

The Provision

First, God provided water by turning a bitter lake into sweet water by having Moses throw in a log. Next, God provided more water by instructing Moses to strike a large rock. When Moses obeyed, the water poured forth.

For food, God provided manna. Like clockwork, each morning, except for the Sabbath, the Israelites awoke to find the bread-like food. The day before the Sabbath, God provided enough for two days.

They had food.

They had water.

God miraculously provided the necessities in such a way that it was unlike any other people group had experienced or known.

When the Israelites ate their fill of manna, they complained and wanted meat. I can relate. God sent quail and they became sick from eating too much.

God provided for the Israelites, for both the short time as they passed through the wilderness, and through the 40 years they wandered that wilderness in punishment.

Knowing that God can cause food to fall on the ground unlike ever before, that He can instantly turn a lake of bitter water into sweet water, that He can make water flow from a rock, and that He can sustain two million people in the wilderness for over 40 years, should tell us that He is quite capable of taking care of you and me.

The Creator and Sustainer of this world has a plan and the ability to provide whatever is needed.

The most comforting passage in understanding how we can trust God to provide is found in Matthew 6:25–33. Jesus makes clear that our Heavenly Father knows what we need. He does. He knew what the Israelites needed in the wilderness. Allow the Lord's words to comfort you: **For the pagans run after all these things, and your heavenly Father knows that you need them (Matthew 6:32, NIV).**

Today's Faith Builder:

Often, the dread of our concerns or fears is worse than reality. Make a list of what you need for the particular task to which you've been called, or even just what you need to survive.

Then ask yourself, "Can God do this?"

DAY 12
Provision of Extra Time

From Joshua 10
The Account of God Providing Extra Time for Israel to Battle the Amorites

The Challenge

My particular calling, or the task I feel called to do right now, is to teach believers about being prepared for any challenge, especially those related to the end times. Creating end-times material and teaching on the topic feels like a race against the clock. My best friend joked with me as I worked on my first book, *Spiritual Prepper*, that the world would end before I finished. And to be fair, it felt like forever.

Whatever the Lord calls each of us to is important to us. We feel the need to get it done fast. Even just walking with the Lord, seeking Him, and trusting Him to provide much-needed provisions is on a time schedule. In life, time is of the essence– whether it's a deadline for a project or a bill that's due. Our needs are often up against a clock.

There's an interesting account of God's provision of time in Joshua 10. This was during the time of the conquest of the Promised Land, as Joshua led his people in battle against the Amorites. The battle raged and the Israelites had the upper hand, but the clock was ticking.

Soon it would be dark.

All their advancement efforts could end in vain.

What were they to do?

Unlike during the Exodus, when Israel departed Egypt, Joshua had experience seeing God provide for every need.

Joshua had lived in the wilderness.

He had witnessed the pillar of fire and the pillar of smoke.

He had eaten the manna and the quail.

He had drunk from the bitter lake and from the rock.

He had already experienced a string of victories in the Promised Land.

As he knew, and we know, God wants his people to cry out to Him and rely on Him. As parents, we want our children to love us, rely on us, follow our lead, and accept the wisdom of our life experience. Even with grown children, we still desire their love, enjoy them seeking our leadership and guidance, and our approval as they make life choices. And we enjoy providing for our children—whether we're providing answers, direction, or provisions. In the same way, God wants us to call upon Him, seek His leadership, His guidance, and desire His will.

In his predicament, it's all Joshua knew to do.

Time was of the essence; victory was on the line. They needed more time—more daylight.

Although Joshua knew God heard the cries of His people and would provide, he had never seen God give extra time. No one had for that matter, not even the angels.

But Joshua trusted in the Lord. He trusted God to give victory, provide, and do the impossible. So, Joshua asked.

The Provision

What did God do?

He pushed the pause button on the sun.

The sun stood still.

Joshua and his army got extra time.

They won the battle.

They completed the mission.

God had provided for their need.

Many of the passages in Scripture that speak of God's provision and of Him taking care of His people, center around a battle, and rightfully so. Though we may not be on a physical battlefield, we're in the midst of a war—a spiritual war. It's a battle to remain faithful in following Christ, and it's a battle to carry out what the Lord has called us to do.

Who would have thought about asking God for extra time?

But who else could help? It's that reality that led the psalmist to write: **Some trust in chariots and some in horses, but we trust in the Name of the Lord our God. They are brought to their knees and fall, but we rise up and stand firm (Psalm 20:7–8, NIV).**

Joshua did not just look to his own strength, nor did he look at the option of losing or at least withdrawing. Joshua knew what God had called them to do. He knew from experience that God would provide if he cried out.

Today's Faith Builder:

Knowing what you need to live, and what is needed to fulfill your calling, it's easy to fear running out of time before the provision arrives. Don't give up. God's timing is perfect in accordance to the big picture.

DAY 13
Provision When Other Things Matter More

From John 6
The Account of Jesus Feeding the Five Thousand

The Challenge

Every king and legendary hero in history had to eat, drink, and rest. No matter what they accomplished, they still required those basic things. Today, national leaders, rock stars, movie stars, and models all must eat, drink, and rest. Everyone needs those most basic elements for survival.

In our walk with Christ, and in ministry, we often focus on the more glamorous, more grandiose aspects. We dream of God using us to lead someone to Him or being used to make a huge impact for Christ.

But in whatever endeavor He calls us, at the end of the day, we still must eat, drink, and sleep.

In John 6, we learn that a crowd of thousands witnessed Jesus performing miracles, healing people, casting out demons, and teaching with authority. They left their towns to gather on a hillside to hear Jesus teach. The recorded five thousand men counted there led some to speculate the number of people to be much greater. Some scholars estimate up to 20,000 people when considering the average number of women and children potentially accompanying each man counted.

For the disciples following Jesus and engaged in His ministry, this was a big moment. This must have seemed glamorous to the disciples—Jesus teaching thousands—and they were a part of the hustle and bustle. The disciples witnessed thousands hearing Jesus, believing Him, and wanting to follow Him. This must have fulfilled their idea of what their Messiah would be like.

Yet, in this big moment, the reality of our human condition rears its head. The disciples heard their stomachs begin to rumble and soon realized others in the crowd were growing antsy. Their empty stomachs begged for attention.

What would they do? The disciples faced a huge crowd—thousands—and they all needed to be fed.

No catering services to be booked.

There was no food except for the lunch of a small boy.

The Provision

Andrew was a man who had confidence in Jesus. He brought the young boy to Jesus, presenting his lunch as all the food found—just five loaves of bread and two fish.

But Jesus performed a miracle.

Jesus not only fed the whole crowd of thousands on that hillside, but the disciples gathered leftovers—12 baskets full to be exact.

God miraculously provided.

He provided for the thousands gathered, the disciples, and even Jesus Himself.

God is fully capable of providing all that is needed. So, no matter what you have done for the Lord, or hope to do, or how glamorous your particular calling may or may not be, you still have core basic needs: eating, drinking, sleeping, and more.

God's not surprised.

As we have already read from Matthew 6:32, God knows your needs.

Jesus makes it clear. As limited human flesh, we need certain things. God the Father knows. Jesus recognized this. Not only did He speak directly to it in Matthew 6:32, but in His model prayer, He asked for daily bread.

So not only does God know what we need, He knows we need it daily.

That is why He sent the manna daily.

Consider the big conference Jesus was holding on the hillside. Teaching and sharing the truth with that crowd was eternally important—like the service you now do for the Lord. But amid important work, Jesus still recognized their basic needs. He does that for us today.

You must know that when you were called to His purpose, Jesus knew what you needed to survive and complete His purpose.

Along with knowing our needs, in Matthew 7:9–11, Jesus says that not only does our Heavenly Father know what we need, but He also wants to give good gifts: "**Which of you, if your son asks for bread, will give him a stone? Or if he asks for a fish, will give him a snake? If you, then, though you are evil, know how** to give good gifts to your children, how much more will your Father in heaven give good gifts to those who ask Him! (Matthew 7:9–11, NIV).

Today's Faith Builder:

Although we know God can provide, and we acknowledge that He knows our needs, we still make up reasons why God wouldn't do that for us in particular. Search your heart. If you feel as if God won't supply your needs, rid yourself of those thoughts.

Choose to believe.

DAY 14
Provision is Yours

From Genesis 22
The Account of God Providing the Sacrifice for Abraham

The Challenge

This section of devotionals on God's provision began with one of the most iconic biblical images: God sending ravens to feed Elijah while he was hidden away in the wilderness. But this wouldn't be an accurate portrayal of God's provision in Scripture without going to the very textual place in which God became known as "Jehovah-Jireh." This name, given to God in Genesis 22 by Abraham, means "The Lord Will Provide."

If you have ever completed a Bible study on the names of God, the name, Jehovah-Jireh, should be familiar. It's important to understand that the name doesn't just mean God provides, it means He *is* the Provider. Abraham previously experienced God's provision long before the events of Genesis 22, but the provision was so significant at that moment that it called for a specific name to define this aspect of God's identity to His people.

The historical account, recorded in Genesis 22, follows a test of faithfulness God presented to Abraham. God instructed Abraham to sacrifice his own son instead of one of the animals normally sacrificed. As an expression of worship, this time it would be his son, Isaac, who'd be laid on an altar, killed, and then burned.

If we don't pause for a moment and think hard on the significance of this act, we miss so much. Abraham's obedience was a big deal to him. Huge. Genesis 22 states that Abraham arose early to obey. He was off to a good start to being faithful.

He took the wood, the knife, the fire, and his son up the mountain. Once there, he built the altar, bound Isaac, and laid him on it. Though a grimacing sight, Abraham was passing the test. Next, he raised the knife and was about to take his son's life.

Comprehend that. He was faithful to the point of giving the life of his son—the promised one—back to God.

That's obedience.

That's faithfulness.

That's trust.

The Provision

Only in those last few seconds did the Angel of the Lord call out, "Abraham, Abraham...don't lay a hand on the boy. Do not do anything to him. Now I know that you fear God, because you have not withheld from me your son, your only son."

Then, there in the brush, was a ram caught by its horns.

That's God's provision.

Like the manna in the wilderness, the water from the rock, and the food brought by ravens—provision miraculously appeared. Abraham responded in worship, recorded in Genesis **22:14, "So Abraham called the name of that place, 'The Lord will**

provide'; as it is said to this day, 'On the mount of the LORD **it shall be provided'" (Genesis 22:14, ESV).**

The declaration Abraham made was an even greater prophetic aspect of provision. For it was also on a hill that God the Father would offer His only Son, Jesus. Jesus was the ultimate provision. His sacrificial death provided forgiveness for our sins.

That's God's sacrificial, eternal, life-saving provision—for *us*.

So, think about your greatest need.

It's the intervention in your life regarding your sin.

For we all have sinned, and that sin eternally separates us from God. It also condemns us to a second death in hell. There's nothing we can do to fix it. We're stuck. As the southern saying goes, that's the greatest pickle we'll ever be in.

But God gave His Son. Jesus paid the price on the cross. He provided for our greatest need. We simply need to believe it and receive it.

As long as we've done that, no matter what needs we encounter, our greatest need has already been met. Our salvation has been provided. Knowing God could meet that need, and did, what could we possibly fear?

When the Lord revealed Himself as the Provider that day on Mount Moriah, it wasn't just about salvation. It set the tone of how God would care for His people. It's not just that God *can* provide—He *will*. And He will provide for you.

Our goal should be to grow Abraham-like confidence in God, the kind demonstrated in this event. He got up early and obeyed. When Isaac questioned the absence of the sacrificial lamb, Abraham said God would provide. In Hebrews 11, we read that Abraham believed that God could raise Isaac from the dead following the sacrifice.

That's faith.

That's confidence in God.

That's trusting God to provide.

God did not fail Abraham. He will not fail you.

Today's Faith Builder:

Settle in your heart that just as God provided for His people in the past, you also will receive His provision.

Week 3

PROTECTION

When God's people have taken a bold stand for Him, even with their lives threatened—He's protected them. Often, when God calls, the mission for His people is daring and dangerous. It also tends to go against the grain of the world. This can put His people in threatening situations. But God has shown repeatedly that He can and will protect His people. There's no limit to the protection He can provide. God will protect His people. He will provide protection for you.

Protection When You're Not to Survive

From Daniel 6
The Account of God Rescuing Daniel from the Lions

The Challenge

Daniel was a distinguished statesman, leading in both the Babylonian Empire and the Persian Empire. With a lifetime of service, Daniel gained the respect of each king, even in their pagan cultures. That was no easy task. Despite being surrounded by paganism, he remained one of the most faithful followers of the One True God in history. Daniel's success and the respect he garnished made him the target of jealousy.

During Daniel's service in the Persian Empire, his fellow governmental administrators became fiercely jealous of him. Eventually having had enough, they plotted how they could leapfrog over him in the chain of command, and how to advance themselves by causing him to fail. Daniel didn't make this easy because his record was impeccable.

Through observing his life, the only thing they presumed might possibly be an Achilles heel was his faith. They knew he followed his God and didn't worship the king, the Persian gods, or idols.

73

His rivals also knew, in Daniel's expression of worship, that he prayed three times a day, facing Jerusalem. They knew that at the time he prayed, Daniel could be seen through an open window. They recognized his faithfulness and loyalty to his God. They knew if they managed to ban such prayer and bowing to someone besides the king, Daniel wouldn't stop.

So, that's what they did.

They set a trap.

They convinced the Persian king to decree that if anyone bowed to any other god, they would be punished unto death. Daniel heard the decree but knew he must remain faithful to the One True God. He also knew God would protect him.

When the time came, Daniel bowed as always, facing Jerusalem with the window open, while with those rivals watched. The men shared the result of their espionage with the king.

Daniel meant so much to this pagan king, that even in this pagan empire, the king spent the day trying to circumvent his own decree.

With no way around it, he had just one choice. Punish Daniel. The king must uphold his word.

Daniel was thrown into what is often referred to as a den of lions. Some commentators describe it as a pen that would've been much like the tomb of Jesus with a stone rolled over the entrance to seal it.

There would be no room for trickery. Daniel would face the lions.

The Provision

Daniel's life of service to the king, and the obvious success God had given Daniel, had made an impact on the king. The Persian king thought God might somehow miraculously save Daniel. First thing the next morning, the king ran to the lions' den and called out to Daniel.

There was an answer.

Daniel was alive.

God had protected him.

Daniel remained faithful and stayed true to his God. And his God rescued. The book of Daniel says that angels were sent to shut the mouths of the lions.

Imagine being Daniel, there in the darkness, feeling the breath and movement of hungry lions, wondering every second if God's protection would remain or run out.

Yet, when the king arrived and saw that Daniel had been spared, he ordered Daniel removed and his accusers thrown in. Before they hit the floor, the lions ripped them apart.

Those lions hadn't been sick or full.

It wasn't a fluke. It wasn't a fault in the lions. It was the provision of protection from the One True God, Daniel's God, who shut their mouths. It was your God—our God—who did that.

Interestingly, close to 400 years before, King David wrote about God shutting the mouth of the lions: **Save me from the mouth of the lion! You have rescued me from the horns of the wild oxen! (Psalm 22:21, ESV)**. David wasn't merely writing poetic words, but he, too, had experienced God's protection from lions. He had told King Saul that he'd killed lions with just a sling and a rock. Benaiah, David's friend and fellow soldier, was also protected when he followed a lion into a pit in the snow and speared it.

Being a man of the Scriptures, it's likely Daniel knew these words, too. He also knew the history of how God had taken care of His people when they took a bold stance. God saw them through time after time.

Daniel knew God protected His people. Know God will provide protection for you, too.

Today's Faith Builder:

Daniel, with a life of faithfulness long before the lion's den, was faithful to pray to the Lord. Commit to begin such a faithful habit.

Protection by a More Reliable Hand

From Genesis 6–8
The Account of God Protecting Noah and His Family

The Challenge

"Why'd you leave all the doors unlocked last night?" I asked my wife. I'd gone to bed before her and had woken up to find all the doors unlocked. We were newly married at the time.

"You're supposed to do that," she replied.

"What? You're the one who went to bed last."

She went on to say that her dad always made sure the doors were locked each night. Neither she nor her mom needed to worry about it. The way I grew up, the last person to bed locked up.

Most conflicts early in a marriage usually arise from different expectations and different childhood experiences. But this isn't a marital devotional book. Believe me, it would be much shorter.

Anyway, I'm sure you understand how my wife felt safe and protected knowing someone made sure the doors were locked.

She may not feel so safe now leaving fallible me in charge of locking all the doors, but what if there was someone omniscient, or infallible, responsible for securing and locking all the doors?

There was that *Someone* in the biblical account of Noah's family and the flood.

In Genesis 6, we read that mankind's wickedness grew so great that God sent a flood upon the earth—a flood so extensive that it left the tallest mountain 20 feet underwater. Only Noah and his family were spared because of Noah's obedience in building an ark according to the detailed specifications God gave him.

For forty days it rained. But there was not just rain. The springs of the great deep burst open. Gushing, rolling, and churning water covered the earth. The waters remained on the earth for 150 days while Noah's family and the creatures within the ark remained in the giant wooden structure. That wooden structure wasn't going to keep them safe all by itself.

The Protection

With that much rain and that much water, how would Noah, his family, and all the animals inside survive? The difference maker was the pitch covering the wooden structure and a door secured and sealed with perfection.

In Genesis 6:14, we read that God instructed Noah to coat the whole ark with pitch—a gummy substance made from pine resin. When applied properly, pitch would provide waterproofing to the wood, cracks, and joints of the ark's construction.

The actual product is not the concern, but the fact that a covering was used is an important theme throughout the Bible. The same word used here to indicate the covering for the ark was also used to indicate the cover of the basket in which Moses was placed. It's also a word picture found in Leviticus indicating the blood of the sacrifice as a "covering" over our sin. It's where we get the idea of atonement.

Therefore, even in the ark, we see a picture of what Jesus' sacrifice on the cross would do—atone for or cover our sins. And like for Noah and his family, that covering would provide salvation.

The other piece of this waterproofing puzzle is in the door. No specifications are given on how a "seal" might be in place to keep the door to the ark from leaking. Nor do we see Noah using human ingenuity to close it. In Genesis 7:16, we read that it was God who closed the door.

That's why it held.

That's why it was waterproof.

That's why Noah and his family survived.

God closed the door.

The One who is all-powerful, all-knowing, and infallible, closed the door.

He shut them in.

He is the One who has shut us into our salvation.

He is the One who is shutting us in through all the storms we may face.

King David, on the receiving end of God's protection and salvation many times, understood God is *the One Reliable Someone* to keep us safe: **My eyes are ever on the Lord, for only He will release my feet from the snare (Psalm 25:15, NIV).**

Today's Faith Builder:

Reflect on times that you've received God's protection—He is reliable, isn't He?

DAY 17
Protection of His and Our Reputations

From 1 Kings 18
*The Account of God Protecting His Own Name Against the
Prophets of Baal*

The Challenge

As a follower of Christ, especially when called to a specific task or mission, failure is a real fear. By publicly professing to be a Christian, publicly making a commitment to a calling, or agreeing to a particular ministry, you may feel as if you've set yourself up for humiliation. What if you can't keep that commitment? What if you can't cut it? If everyone knows you've committed, surely everyone will see you fail.

Yikes.

These thoughts run wild, each bouncing off one side of our brains and propelling into the other, feeding our fears. What we must understand is that it's not our reputation on the line. It's God's.

God's Name is on the line, not ours.

The kingdom of Israel led by Saul, David, and Solomon was split following Solomon's death. The ten tribes in the North took the name, Israel. The two in the South, Judah. Both nations turned away from God and turned toward idols. They both turned to the gods of the neighboring nations. Israel especially so.

It was the calling of the prophets to warn and admonish the people back to faithfulness, but Scripture tells us that the prophets were hated and often killed. They were despised.

Elijah was one of those prophets. His charge was to speak the truth to Israel, under the rule of King Ahab and his wife, Jezebel, in the time of their greatest wickedness and idolatry.

Following God's direction, Elijah challenged the prophets of one of the gods worshipped by Israel—Baal. Elijah had Ahab send for all the people of Israel to come watch this challenge on Mt. Carmel.

The people came, along with 450 prophets of Baal. The 450 prophets were challenged to build an altar on which to place a bull. Elijah would do the same. Each would stand before their altars and pray to their respective gods. Whichever sent fire to burn the bull would prove to be the true god. Raising the challenge up a notch, Elijah soaked his altar with water.

Elijah was confident, but his reputation as being a true prophet was on the line. For one, to be a prophet of Yahweh required 100% accuracy. Not only was his reputation on the line, but Ahab and Jezebel wanted him dead. The thousands gathered there wanted him dead. The 450 prophets wanted him dead.

What a challenge.

450 to 1.

Before a nation and outnumbered.

His reputation on the line.

His life on the line.

The 450 prophets prayed, begged, and performed ceremonial practices toward their god.

The Victory

Those prophets—the prophets of Baal—only heard silence.

Elijah prayed.

Boom.

God sent fire from Heaven.

The bull was burned, and the wood, and the stones, and all the water.

God proved Himself to be above all.

Elijah's reputation was saved. His vindication was much like what King David experienced and wrote about in a psalm: **No one who hopes in You will ever be put to shame (Psalm 25:3a, NIV).**

Elijah wasn't put to shame. His reputation was protected because it wasn't just Elijah's reputation on the line—it was God's also. It's the same for us when we stand for Him.

Today's Faith Builder:

Think about your walk with the Lord. You represent Him. He will not let His reputation be harmed.

DAY 18
Protection When Outnumbered

From 2 Kings 6
The Account of God Protecting Elisha with an Angel Army

The Challenge

Living counterculturally. Going against the flow. Taking steps of faith that defy logic and the wisdom of this world. All can leave us feeling alone.

We may feel outnumbered.

This is something faithful followers of God have often felt—and more than that, they've often experienced it physically.

The prophet Elisha and his servant faced this reality. Israel, at war with Aram, remained one step ahead of them. The king of Aram grew angry and threatened his officers because he was convinced a spy existed among them in their own ranks.

There wasn't a spy.

God was giving Elisha the plans of the Arameans and Elisha was warning Israel's king.

Upon learning this, the Aramean king sent orders for his army to surround the city where Elisha was staying. A large number of soldiers, horses, and chariots gathered at night. The next morning, Elisha's servant stepped outside and saw the city surrounded. The size and strength of the force he saw terrified him. He ran in to tell Elisha.

A servant and prophet were no match for this army.

The Protection

Elisha didn't flinch. His confidence in God remained unshaken. Instead, he prayed for the servant's eyes to be opened.

God opened the servant's eyes and allowed him to see beyond the physical realm. He looked in the hills around the city and saw a much larger angel army with horses and chariots of fire.

The Aramean army faced more than just Elisha and his servant.

God had it covered. He showed up to take care of His servants.

A psalm captures the reality of all who follow the Lord: **As for God, His way is perfect: The Lord's word is flawless; He shields all who take refuge in Him (Psalm 34:10, NIV).**

Pause a moment. Recognize the confidence we can have in God's protection simply based on the knowledge that His works happen all around us—though we may not see. That alone is encouraging enough, but the story doesn't stop there. As it continues, we're given an account that displays God's power and His humor.

Following the eyes of Elisha's servant being opened, Elisha prayed that the eyes of the Arameans would be closed— that they would be blinded. They were.

Elisha then met the army as they came after him. He told them they weren't on the right road nor the right city to catch the man they sought to kill. He then offered to show them the way. Elisha led the enemy of Israel marching into Israel's capital, Samaria, and directly to the king.

This account marks one of the most humiliating defeats of an army in history and in Scripture—particularly given how much they had outnumbered Israel. Wow. Imagine that.

God protected His servant, Elisha.

God will protect you.

And following Christ, you're never alone.

Today's Faith Builder:

The best response to today's devotion is to do what Elisha did—pray. Pray for your eyes to be opened and reframe your mindset.

DAY 10
Protection in Obedience

From Daniel 3
The Account of God Protecting in the Fiery Furnace

The Challenge

In the Psalms, God is referred to as our shield, fortress, and refuge. This is because, throughout the lives of David and other psalmists, God protected them. And as we've repeatedly seen throughout this week of devotions—God protects His people.

Our invincible God is fully capable of protecting us against all sorts of odds. He is attentive to our lives to know when we need to be rescued. He often intercedes, mercifully and gracefully offering protection, even when we're in rebellion to Him, though He's not bound to do so. He promises to protect us when we're faithfully pursuing His Will and are obeying His Word. He promises supernatural protection when we stand for Him. This protection may not always look the way we would draw it. Being invincible under God's protection doesn't mean we walk away from trouble unscathed, or even alive. For us as believers, the age to come far outweighs this life. The bumps, bruises, and brokenness we face along the way are often for the best in our lives, and they are most certainly for God's glory. Though His

89

protection may not come as we imagine, we can be certain that He will be with us.

In Daniel 3, during the reign of King Nebuchadnezzar in Babylon, we see in Scripture a great example of how God works in the lives of His faithful when they face fiery trials.

Ahead of the larger population of Judah being exiled to Babylon, young men of Judah's nobility were carried away to Babylon. The noble sons of Judah were put in the court of the king to be trained in the Babylonian way of life and leadership. The most famous of these captives was Daniel, who experienced the incredible hand of God's protection when thrown into the lions' den.

Scripture gives us the names of three more of these young men: Shadrach, Meshach, and Abednego. Like Daniel, they were in governmental service in Babylon. All the king's officials assembled for the dedication of an enormous gold statue of Nebuchadnezzar. Everyone was instructed to bow and worship the statue when the music played. Any who refused would be thrown into a hot furnace.

The music played.

The officials bowed.

The three young men stood.

They would not bow before another god or an image of a god.

They were faithful, but would God protect them?

The Protection

It didn't seem so, at first.

They were seized.

They were bound in the furnace.

The furnace was turned up seven times hotter—so hot that the soldiers who bound the men were killed.

Surely, since they were so bold and so faithful, God would keep them from being placed in the furnace. Surely, He would not allow the temperature to be turned up seven times hotter.

He did.

But unlike the soldiers, the three men did not die.

As the king and the crowd looked on, Shadrach, Meshach, and Abednego walked around in the furnace unbound and unharmed.

Another sight perplexed the king.

There were not just three men in the fire, but four. The fourth looked like the Son of God.

Three young men were thrown into the fire but were protected.

They had been faithful, and God kept His promise.

This was a promise David knew well and wrote in the well-known Psalm 23: **I will fear no evil, for you are with me (Psalm 23:4, NIV).**

As read in a previous devotional, Jesus gave this same promise. He promised to be with His followers even unto the end of the age. And that includes the fire.

The Lord was with Shadrach, Meshach, and Abednego in the furnace.

He is with us now.

Today's Faith Builder:

Don't just think of your circumstances. Think of the One who will be with you in them and through them.

DAY 20
Protection Against the Uncontrollable

From Matthew 8, Mark 4, & Luke 8
The Account of Jesus Stopping the Wind

The Challenge

Most all the disciples were fishermen and had spent their lives on the water of the Sea of Galilee. They knew the water. They knew boats. They knew how to navigate through difficult conditions.

Much of Jesus' three years of ministry, and therefore the three years of discipling the apostles, took place around the Sea of Galilee. In the Gospels, we find them often in boats.

There's no doubt they'd experienced bad weather and rough water before, but even with this lifetime of experience, there came a night in which they were terrified. Matthew, Mark, and Luke tell of the intense storm that came upon them. Jesus was asleep and the disciples were freaking out. There were strong winds and high waves. The boat was taking on water, perhaps to the point of sinking. The Gospel accounts tell us it was dangerous. These fishermen had real cause for concern. Their assessment of the conditions was legitimate.

Surely, they'd tried all they could, whether that was scooping out water, paddling faster, or changing directions. With their knowledge, they would have tried everything. The situation was dire, and they had no control over what happened next.

The Protection

Jesus slept through all the chaos. They woke Him. And told Him their fears.

Jesus spoke not to the disciples, but to the wind and the waves.

"Quiet. Be still!"

He rebuked the waves and the wind.

The disciples were left stunned.

I wonder what they believed waking Jesus up would accomplish. They'd witnessed Him perform other miracles, but from their comments following the waves and wind ceasing, that wasn't what they thought Jesus would do.

Maybe they thought He'd make the water evaporate out of the boat.

Maybe they thought He'd speed the boat to the shore.

I don't know.

There were aspects of this situation that were more controllable than others.

The waves and the wind seemed out of the question to be controlled, yet Jesus rebuked them and stopped them. The waves and the wind listened and obeyed.

The disciples voiced their astonishment in Mark 4:41: **"Who is this? Even the wind and the waves obey Him!" (Mark 4:41, NIV).**

It's no mistake that the challenges we face in our individual lives are often called storms. They bring damage like storms. They're often beyond our control, leaving us at their mercy. We're left in the proverbial boat—taking on water, terrified, and wondering why God hasn't stepped in and saved the day.

If He can speak to the uncontrollable waves and wind, God can rebuke anything you are facing or will face. If He can stop waves and wind, He can stop the storm crashing down on your life. Just as Jesus was in the boat with the disciples, He's with us. Before His death, He even told the disciples that it was best for Him to ascend to Heaven so that the Holy Spirit could come and indwell all believers.

Through the Holy Spirit, we have God dwelling in us.

As Jesus told the disciples, and as it's been repeated many times in this book, He is with us until the end of the age.

Yes, the One who stopped the uncontrollable is with us. He's with you.

Today's Faith Builder:

Look at the life storms bearing down on you and ask yourself if you've accepted that they will just continue because no one can help. If so, reframe your thinking because Jesus can.

DAY 21
Protection is Yours

From Exodus 12
The Account of God Protecting the Firstborn of the Israelites

The Challenge

My grandpa and uncles raced dirt track cars when I was younger. I enjoyed watching them race. I remember sitting in the grandstands with my family and overhearing my grandma regularly being asked if she worried about my grandpa or her sons racing. She always offered the same reply. She didn't worry. Why didn't she? She always said it was because a race car was one of the safest places someone could be.

Now that's not entirely accurate—there have been many fatalities in racing. However, this number isn't remotely close to the number of deaths attributed to daily driving—driving that even includes trips to the grocery store. What my grandma meant when she touted the safety of a race car was that every measure had been taken to ensure the safety of the driver.

Race cars are built to protect the racer in collisions, rollovers, fires, and any other possibility. From head to toe, racers like my Papaw were covered in fireproof gear—shoes, gloves, and fire suits. They wore helmets and neck braces, had special seats and harnesses—all designed for safety. Even racetracks are constantly being improved for safety.

Before modern airbags, seatbelt safety laws, and the sophisticated camera systems of today, the design of race cars far surpassed safety measures of the family vehicle. Even today, in our uber-safe world, it can still be more dangerous to drive to the grocery store than to be in a race car.

I think about what my Nana would say when I think about following Christ. I have friends who are missionaries in places I can't share. To do so would compromise their lives. They're living and ministering in war zones, and in places where it's illegal to be a Christian or share the Gospel. Many of them serve there with their children.

Through years as a student pastor, I've had students commit their lives to missions. I've had conversations with terrified parents who were fearful their children would end up in those dangerous places.

But let's go back to what my Nana would say. She didn't worry about my Papaw or uncles, because all possible measures were taken to keep them safe. Therefore, a race car was a safe place even when going fast and racing hard. To that same degree (and more), being wherever the Lord may lead—whether you're a family on the mission field, a believer in a highly persecuted area, or if your child is called to a place that terrifies you—that's still the safest place one can be.

Please understand this. God protecting us when we follow Him doesn't mean we won't face danger or difficulties. But God is invincible and, when we follow Him, we can trust we're invincible unto the mission to which He calls us.

The promised protection we've discussed this past week is meant to be understood through Matthew 10:28: "Do not be afraid of those who kill the body but cannot kill the soul. Rather, be afraid of the One who can destroy both soul and body in hell."

When we accept the sacrifice Jesus made on the cross, and receive His salvation, we never need to fear the worst. We live each day with nothing to lose, for the age to come will far exceed even the best we could hope for now. But God's protection extends into this physical life and, often out of mercy, extends protection to even His people who have strayed.

We find promises such as Matthew 6:33, where if we seek Him first, He will take care of us. But the greatest display of this promise and reality is found in the account of the Passover. When Pharaoh wouldn't allow Israel to leave, God sent a plague upon Egypt in which every firstborn would die.

Often when retold, we indicate the plaque targeted the Egyptians, but in reality, it wasn't only the Egyptians. Firstborns would be lost in all households that did not follow God's instructions. This included the Israelites, though we have no record that any of them disobeyed.

The Lord's instruction was to sacrifice a lamb and place its blood on their doorpost. In doing so, the Angel of Death would pass over that home. Each Israelite family faced a challenge. Would they take cover under the blood of a lamb or not?

The Protection

Those who took that step of faith kept their firstborn alive and family intact. It's a picture of how God continues to protect.

You have the opportunity for that same protection.

If you accept whatever the Lord calls you to do—you will be protected.

It's easy to read or listen to the stories of "heroes" of the faith and believe in God's provision of protection for them but doubt it to be true for you. However, it *is* true for you.

The lamb's blood on the doorpost was a foreshadowing of the ultimate sacrifice to come nearly 1500 years later. We are all targets of the second death because of the fall of man in the Garden of Eden. Our destiny in the age to come would be hell if not for the intervention made in Jesus' death on the cross, and our accepting it by faith.

If you have received that sacrifice by faith, then you are protected from the future judgment and wrath of God. You're protected from hell. Is there any greater protection that can be offered?

It's crazy. We accept God's supernatural protection in this manner, but then doubt He'll protect us in the lesser struggles of each day. How foolish of us.

God protects His people.

God protects you.

We need to think about Him as our protection as in Psalm 27: **For in the day of trouble He will keep me safe in His dwelling; He will hide me in the shelter of His sacred tent and set me high upon a rock (Psalm 27:5, NIV).**

Today's Faith Builder:

Reflect on the protection given through the cross.

Week 4

IMPOSSIBLE

In almost every instance when God has given victory, provision, or protection for His people in Scripture, that feat or miracle was done when His people faced an impossible situation. The path on which God leads His followers often runs up against the most impossible challenges. Fortunately for us, His people, God makes the impossible possible. He will make the impossible possible for you.

DAY 22
Impossible Predicament Made Possible

From Exodus 13 & 14
The Account of God Parting the Red Sea

The Impossible Challenge

Once you complete this 40-day devotional, it's my hope that you gain a bigger, clearer view of God. In addition, it's important that you gain an understanding of just how much God cares for you. Though He sustains the universe, He also knows the small details of your life.

Each week is a new division in this 40-day journey. We've looked at how, in Christ, we're invincible, victorious, provided for, and protected. In these categories, there's a lot of overlap.

In victory, there is going to be provision and protection. In protection there's victory and so on. In each of these divisions you've read, each account shows God giving victory, providing, or protecting against the impossible. That's what separates God from anyone or anything else—He conquers the impossible. Generation after generation of His people has watched Him make the impossible possible in supernatural, mind-blowing ways.

But even with such a supernatural body of work, God's people tend to forget about His miracles. For some reason, they think their situation is different than the wonders He's done in the past.

I've done it.

You've probably done it.

When are we going to get it?

When are we going to just have faith and trust Him, even if we're against unfathomable odds?

He can do it.

He has done it.

God is invincible, and He's invincible even against the impossible.

That's why this week focuses on pointing out when God gave victory, brought provision, or protected His people in the most impossible of predicaments.

But we need to remember what He has already done and realize that what He's done before, He can do again.

Throughout the Old Testament, especially through the oracles given by the prophets, Israel was instructed to remember all God had done. This is a constant reminder from the prophets. But still, immediately after certain events, God's people were instructed to erect memorials so they would remember.

In particular, God's people were told to remember the Exodus. They were told to remember how, when enslaved in Egypt, God heard their cries and came down to rescue them. They were instructed to remember how He sent Moses to convince Pharaoh to let the Israelites go and how Pharaoh refused. They were told to always recall how God sent ten supernatural plagues, and how Pharaoh finally relented and let the people go.

Following the Israelites' release, during their journey through the wilderness, God repeatedly produced miracle after miracle to care for His people. You've already read many of those feats earlier in this book.

In the series of God's miraculous events throughout Exodus, one moment stands above the rest. It's the fulcrum of Israel's history. It leveraged them into becoming the nation God promised them to be. It was a feat the nation was constantly told to remember.

It was after the Passover and the loss of his own firstborn when Pharaoh finally gave the Hebrews their freedom. This group of thousands, and quite possibly more than a million, left the land of the Nile and headed through the wilderness. They followed the pillar of fire at night and the pillar of smoke by day. If you remember from an earlier devotional, this provided both direction and timing. If the people kept pace, they would remain in God's will and on His path.

While the Israelites were still in the wilderness, Pharaoh's heart hardened again. He changed his mind and sent his chariots after them. Following the God-provided navigation pillars, the Israelites arrived on an area of the beach by the Red Sea. It was perfect for setting up camp, but not for defending a nation against the most powerful army on Earth at the time. Rugged cliffs draped the sides of the beach with the Red Sea before them. Behind them raced Pharaoh's Army. The Hebrews were penned like lambs led to slaughter.

No place to go.

No place to hide.

The moment was bleak.

There was reasonable cause for the murmuring of the Israelites, as many said it would have been better if they'd been left in slavery.

There was no escape.

They were trapped.

The predicament was impossible.

The Impossible Made Possible

At that moment, the Lord told Moses to lift up his staff. When Moses obeyed, God performed one of the most iconic miracles in biblical history. Before them, the Red Sea parted and produced a highway of dry land in which to cross the sea. Walls of water stood on both sides. Thousands and thousands of people hurried across. Everyone made it.

God had performed another rescue, but for a period of time, it looked as if He was failing. Egyptian chariots reached the path God provided for the Hebrews and they, too, began to cross the sea. They were closing in on Israel. Much of the army made it onto the path through the sea. Then God did something else.

He released the wall of water and the sea crashed down upon the chariots.

God's people were safe.

With its army depleted, Egypt would be unable to cause Israel much trouble ahead.

This was the impossible predicament God made possible—the one He constantly urged His people to remember and reflect upon.

This event can be pictured in Psalm 27:3: **Though an army besiege me, my heart will not fear; though war break out against me, even then I will be confident (Psalm 27:3, NIV)**. This is the confidence we're meant to gain.

Today's Faith Builder:

Again, remember the victories God has given you in the past, and reflect upon them.

DAY 23

Impossible Was Created

From Genesis 1 & 2
The Account of God Creating Everything

The Impossible Challenge

What do you believe is the most amazing feat of God?

That's tough to decide. There's a long list of His works to consider. We've read up to 22 at this point, and we're just scratching the surface of what is recorded in Scripture. There's so much more we don't even know. The apostle John wrote in his Gospel that Jesus did so much more than what was recorded. That's a statement each Bible author could have written. God does and has done so much that we can't even grasp, much less find a way to put into words.

From the list of miracles we know about, the greatest feat perhaps comes down to the creation of this world.

Think with me in terms of God's ability to make the impossible possible in relation to His creating the universe. That thought alone should put to rest any doubts about God, and any talk about anything He can't do. Consider this: Any task, situation, or challenge we label "impossible" was created by God. The impossible situation had to come about from some series of origins, and the ultimate origin is God.

111

Wrap your head around that.

In high school, I took guitar lessons from an elderly gentleman who'd had a career in the music industry. He offered bits of wisdom during the lessons.

Once, as I struggled with a song, he pointed to the sheet music and said, "You see that music. Do you see a name on it? That was the songwriter. He was a man [human], not something out of this world. If a song was written by a man, then it can be played by a man."

That's an interesting bit of wisdom, right?

I held on to that and have tried to apply it to every difficult thing I have faced.

I'm not sure if the song was "Twinkle, Twinkle Little Star" or "Home on the Range." Both gave me troubles. And I'm pretty sure I never mastered "Home on the Range," but when things get tough, sometimes it's those words that keep me pressing on.

Let's look at them from a different perspective for a bit. If something was created by a person, then that person would have no problem solving the situation, mastering the challenge, or finishing the task. The creator of the thing could do it.

So, wouldn't that also be true for the One who created everything?

And since God created everything, He is quite capable of everything. Since we are His people, created by Him, He is quite able and capable of helping us in any situation.

Let's break this down to the simplest illustration. Consider a treasure hunt or an Easter egg hunt. When the hunt is over and there is still treasure or an egg left to find, who do you ask where it can be found?

Right! You'd ask the one who hid it—the one who "created" the hunt.

As a follower of Christ, we belong to and are following the One who made everything.

There is nothing we should fear.

In this context, there's nothing that is impossible. What is created by God, can be accomplished by God.

Nothing—N O T H I N G—is beyond His reach or abilities.

To add to this strong feat, God had nothing before Him when He made the Earth. It was made from nothing. It's also important to note that He spoke it into existence.

Think about this impossibility...

> Now the earth was formless and empty, darkness was over the surface of the deep, and the Spirit of God was hovering over the waters (Genesis 1:2, NIV).

Nothing.

A void.

A blank canvas.

The Impossible Made Possible

Then God spoke.

God said, "Let there be light," and there was light (Genesis 1:3).

He kept speaking until this world was made.

All that we know was spoken into existence from nothing (except man, whom God formed with His hands, but that's another matter).

Sounds impossible.

As Creator, He made it all, and it's all His. **The earth is the Lord's, and everything in it, the world, and all who live in it (Psalm 24:1, NIV).**

Today's Faith Builder:

Whatever seems impossible, ask yourself who created the elements of the situation.

DAY 24
Impossible Proof Made Possible

From 2 Kings 20
The Account of God Giving a Proof of Healing to Hezekiah

The Impossible Challenge

We often can believe in God and believe we're invincible, victorious, provided for, and protected by Him. We can believe He is capable and willing to take care of us. We can even have believed in God for years and still come to one particular promise from God that is difficult to accept—whether it is a biblical promise that applies to our current condition or a personal utterance received in our spirit.

For example, the Bible says God will provide, but perhaps you struggle to believe that promise regarding a recent job loss. Or perhaps you received a difficult diagnosis, and through prayer, you felt assured by the Holy Spirit that you'd be healed, but nevertheless, you have doubt. We often can have great faith, but still struggle in specific instances.

By doing so, we're not any different than many heroes in the Bible, including a hero like King Hezekiah. Hezekiah was a good king of Judah. He faithfully followed God and accomplished great things. We've already read of his faith when Jerusalem was under siege. He took the letter from the Assyrian commander and laid it before God, seeking God to rescue the city.

Later in life, the king became deathly ill. The prophet Isaiah was sent to tell him that he would not recover and would die from this illness. Isaiah left and Hezekiah cried out to the Lord.

The Impossible Made Possible

Isaiah had barely left when the Lord gave a new prognosis. The prophet was instructed to return and give the king a new report. He relayed the message God had given him: "I have heard your prayer and seen your tears...I will add fifteen years to your life."

Hezekiah had been granted a longer life. He had been healed. There, God delivered the impossible, miraculously circumventing Hezekiah's death.

Consider this—that feat was not the most impossible-made-possible thing of God.

A lesson on faith can found in Hezekiah's prayer, but that's not the point we're looking for here. Although Hezekiah had been a man of faith and had prayed for healing in faith, this answer of faith was still hard to accept.

He asked for a sign. A difficult sign—the sun moving backward.

This had never happened before.

It had been stopped once however, and King Hezekiah would have known that from Joshua's account.

But backward?

Again, no big deal for God. No big deal for the Creator. No big deal for the Invincible One.

Seemingly, immediately it happened. The God who made the sun and mapped out its path sent it backward.

An impossible proof was made possible.

Yes, this sign was for Hezekiah, but it is for us, also.

It was a sign to stand the ages, just as all the feats mentioned in this book. They point to a God who is bigger than we can even comprehend—and He cares for us more than we can imagine.

A God who can make the impossible possible.

A God who is invincible and can make His people invincible.

We can trust God for He is quite capable of doing the impossible. He's proven it. We already knew He could stop the sun and hold it in place. In this passage in 2 Kings 20, we learned that not only could He move it backward but could move it ahead.

In Psalm 147, the psalmist reflects on all he personally experienced God do, along with all the impossible-made-possible feats God accomplished up to that point. He writes, **Great is our Lord and mighty in power; His understanding has no limit (Psalm 147:5, NIV).**

This is our God. He is limitless.

Today's Faith Builder:

You're trusting the Lord for something particular. Trust what He has said. He's given us proof time after time.

Impossible Solution Made Possible

From Luke 1 & 2
The Account of God Bringing the Savior into the World

The Impossible Challenge

In Genesis 3:15, we find what is called the protoevangelium which means "the first Gospel" or "the first Good News." More clearly, it can be understood as the first prophecy of the Messiah. It's the first prophecy that God would send a Savior into the world. This prophecy comes after Adam and Eve sinned in the Garden of Eden. Amid pronouncing their punishment, along with the curses upon the world and the serpent, the Lord proclaimed,

> *And I will put enmity between you [the serpent] and the woman, and between your [seed] and hers; He will crush your head, and you will strike His heel* (Genesis 3:15, NIV).

From this early time, God revealed He had a plan to solve mankind's sin problem—a Savior would be sent. An Anointed One. The Lord revealed what He would one day do. This first prophecy was 4,000 years before Jesus' incarnation.

Throughout the unfolding of the Scripture, prophets continued this narrative of the anticipated Savior, the promised

119

Son of David. He would solve man's problem of sin and establish an eternal kingdom from Jerusalem.

The unfolding of Scripture also revealed the apparent need for a solution to the sin problem. Our sin separates us from God and sentences us to the second death—the lake of fire. Sin prevents us from enjoying eternal life in God's kingdom.

A solution was necessary.

It had been promised.

Throughout the 4,000 years prior to the Savior's earthly arrival, God set very specific and restrictive methods for the atonement of man's sin. So, to have a once-and-for-all sacrifice —the sacrifice of all sacrifices—it would be particularly specific as to who, what, when, where, and how. Everything God said through the biblical writers had to be fulfilled completely— every specific detail and restriction.

One major restriction required a pure and blameless sacrifice to atone for our sins. In terms of the solution being a person, that person had to be without sin.

As humans, we become sinful in two ways. First, we inherit sin from Adam. It is understood that sin is passed through men to their offspring, beginning with Adam. We're guilty because of the sin nature we inherited. Second, we are unrighteous because we sin. It doesn't take much to prove that if we walked in Adam's bare feet, we'd make the same mistake in the Garden.

Since all are physically born as descendants of Adam, no one can be born free of original sin.

This creates a multi-layer problem that calls for a multi-layered solution.

How then, could a perfect, sinless Savior be born?

The Lord revealed the answer in Genesis 3:15, but for that to happen seemed impossible.

That's what the young girl, Mary, said when the angel, Gabriel, appeared to her.

He told her she had found favor with God and would have a son. He would be great. The Son of God. The promised Son of David. The Messiah. The Christ. The Savior. The promised solution.

It wasn't a lapse of faith, but confusion that lead Mary to reply, "How will this be since I'm a virgin?"

A good question.

It was impossible for someone to have a child as a virgin.

It was also impossible for a child to be born without sin if the mother was not a virgin.

The Impossible Made Possible

God had a plan—Gabriel explained how the Lord would miraculously give a child to a virgin.

God also had a plan on how to circumvent the inheritance of a sinful nature—by Jesus, the Son of God, taking on flesh and dwelling among us.

Gabriel told Mary, **"For nothing will be impossible with God" (Luke 1:37, ESV).** Nothing is impossible with God—not even a virgin birth or a sinless sacrifice.

A virgin birth happened. On a journey to register for the census, Mary still a virgin, gave birth to Jesus in Bethlehem.

A sinless sacrifice happened. Jesus went to the cross without sin. His sacrificial death atoned for our sin. The impossible solution became possible. Part of the first prophecy was fulfilled and the serpent managed to get in a strike. But at Jesus' return, the second part will be fulfilled: Jesus will crush Satan and establish His own kingdom.

Today's Faith Builder:

God had a plan all along for the most difficult dilemma in history. It's been nearly 6,000 years, and He's still working that plan. Trust that He's at work right now in your life.

DAY 26

Impossible Stroll Made Possible

From Mark 6
The Account of Jesus Walking on the Water

The Impossible Challenge

Over the process of writing this book, I made a point of asking kids their favorite feat of God, or favorite story of Jesus. There's one story they mention far more than any others. Of all the supernatural miracles of Jesus, this seems least purposeful. It's almost as if Jesus did it just because He could.

While children often repeat this story, it is one of the most noted accounts of Jesus among nonbelievers. They may not know the wonder of the cross, but they know the impossible feat of walking on water.

Maybe that was the point. Jesus knew what would resonate with people across the world throughout the ages.

This miracle has transcended the ages indeed.

It's a unique story. Jesus had been teaching on a hillside on the bank of the Sea of Galilee. During that teaching, He fed 5,000 with five loaves of bread and two fish. As the crowds were dispersing, Jesus sent the disciples on ahead, so they loaded into the boat with their twelve baskets of leftovers. Like the stories in this book, a testimony of faith lay at their feet—all around them, in fact.

Jesus spent time in prayer. Finishing His prayer, Jesus observed the disciples making little headway against the wind, leaving them nearly stalled in the middle of the sea. They were a long way from Jesus.

At three o'clock in the morning, He went to help.

The Impossible Made Possible

Did Jesus take a boat?

No.

He walked.

He walked on water.

He defied the laws of gravity, and laws of water, too.

As He neared them, the disciples cried out, believing that Jesus was a ghost. He was walking on water, after all. Yes, water. He spoke to them and told them to not be afraid. Then He got into the boat with them.

This impossible stroll is another wonderful piece of evidence that Jesus is the Son of God. It once again proved there was something special about Him. It served as a reminder that the disciples were called to make disciples all around the world. And it reminded them that Jesus said He'd be with them. Because Jesus, the One capable of walking on water, is capable of anything.

Saving them physically was not the point. The point was to build their faith—to build their trust and confidence in Him. In Mark 6:52, it's indicated that the disciples feared because they had not comprehended the miracle of the five loaves and two fish.

While not clearly stated, it's implied that the disciples should not have been afraid. Why? Because Jesus, the Son of God, the Messiah, the One who healed and performed miracles had just turned two fish and five loaves of bread into food for at least 5,000. And He was the One who had sent them on the mission in the boat. He, the Performer of Miracles, sent them.

He was the One capable of controlling waves and wind.

They were going to be fine—no matter what appeared before them.

Such faith seems impossible—to trust Jesus' protection so much so that what appears to be a ghost strolling along in the middle of the sea fails to incite even a flinch in fear.

The Bible is full of followers of Christ who remained fearless and trustful in far more dangerous situations. Stephen prayed for those stoning him as he died. Paul said he remained content in all situations. That was faith. He said to die was gain. He felt complete faith in Jesus.

Others have grown to this point.

We can, too.

We should.

How? Because Jesus walked on water and promised to be with us until the end of the age.

Jesus can be counted on. **Our help is in the name of the LORD, the Maker of heaven and earth (Psalm 24:1, NIV).**

Today's Faith Builder:

Like the disciples, you have reminders of God's provision and protection at your feet. Grasp the message. Cling to it.

DAY 27
Impossible Reality Made Possible

From John 11
The Account of Jesus Raising Lazarus from the Dead

The Impossible Challenge

During His time on Earth in the first advent, Jesus built personal relationships.

He had friends. Dear friends.

Nothing has changed, the Lord is personable.

Three of Jesus' dear friends were Mary, Martha, and Lazarus. Two sisters and a brother. We find their paths crossing with Jesus often. One intersection was via a letter Jesus received. Mary and Martha sent word that their brother, Jesus' friend, was terribly sick. They wrote, "Lord, behold, he whom You love is sick." As revealed later in the account, they expected Jesus to heal him. They knew He could.

Here's the scene. Lazarus is home in Bethany near Jerusalem, deathly ill. His sisters are with him. They know its terminal. They also realize they can't do anything. They're upset. They're distraught. The only possible remedy would be Jesus' healing, something they had personally witnessed numerous times.

Jesus was an estimated 90 miles northeast of Bethany. John's account simply states that they got word to Jesus, but as we would be, they must have been hoping for their brother to be rescued.

They knew that Jesus, their friend, the Messiah, could do it.

The account also reveals Jesus likely had supernatural knowledge of Lazarus' condition. In John 11:11–14, He states that Lazarus has died. This revelation to the Twelve came after Jesus received the letter of Lazarus' sickness two days prior. Jesus made a conscious decision to stay in Perea two more days rather than beginning the four-day journey.

A seemingly odd decision. But Jesus knew what He was doing.

Finally, after the two-day wait and the four-day journey, Jesus arrives in Bethany. Mary stays home while Martha runs out to meet Jesus. She is still holding out hope for the impossible: "Lord, if You had been here, my brother would not have died. But even now I know that whatever You ask of God, God will give You."

It would seem that being friends with Jesus would make them invincible, but Lazarus now lay as a smelly corpse locked in a tomb for four days.

The Impossible Made Possible

Four days, certified dead. In physical reality, Lazarus' life was over. Still, Jesus said, "Roll the stone away."

Still, Jesus said, "Lazarus, come out!"

Still, Jesus said, "Take off the grave clothes and let him go."

Lazarus was dead, and the dead resurrecting seemed impossible.

But with the Lord, there are no impossibilities.

Jesus raised Lazarus from the dead.

Jesus made clear over and over in this account that His waiting had a purpose. He waited so they would recognize Him as the Christ, know that God is truly powerful, and strengthen their faith.

Jesus orchestrated this display of power because their faith was of greater importance than momentary suffering or pain. To grow them to invincible faith, He showed them God's power to even overcome death itself.

This applies to us. It's unlikely our loved ones won't be called out of tombs right now. But, if they have trusted in Christ, one day they will. And so will we. Death does not and will not win.

But as in this account, timing is important, and pain is allowed—all for the sake of increasing faith and glorifying God. This is the core of our invincibility. We can trust God no matter the strength of the storms in our lives. Though we may not be spared the hurt, we can know He's accomplishing something greater and bigger in us and through the situation. We're invincible because Jesus has already won.

God takes the impossible reality and makes it possible.

This account makes clear that God works behind the scenes for those who love Him. **And we know that in all things**

God works for the good of those who love Him, who have been called according to His purpose (Romans 8:28, NIV).

Today's Faith Builder:

Jesus received Mary and Martha's letter. He gets your letters (prayers), too.

DAY 28
Your Impossible Challenge Made Possible

From Book of You Chapter Now
The Account of God Making Your Impossible Challenge Possible

Your Impossible Challenge

With 28 days in, it's time to ask a few questions. Do you feel an increase in your believing? Has your confidence in God grown? Are you feeling more strength in your faith? We hope so.

All these truths are important, but unless they penetrate your heart and connect with your life, these lessons are just words. At the end of each week, we turn to your life and give you an opportunity to reflect. Not only can you see that heroes of faith are invincible in the Lord, but you can be, too. In your own walk with Christ, you will be victorious. He will provide. He will protect. And yes, He'll make the impossible possible.

Let's do a faith-building exercise so that you know whether or not you're connecting these principles to your life. Today, you will help us write the devotional.

What's your current challenge or challenges?

_____

_____

_____

_____

_____

_____

_____

_____

_____

What makes this challenge or these challenges
impossible?

_____

_____

_____

_____

_____

_____

_____

_____

_____

Your Impossible Made Possible

What attribute (characteristic) of God encourages you
in this impossible challenge? (Appendix 4 could help.)

_____

_____

_____

What promise from God encourages you in this impossible challenge?

_____

_____

_____

What act, miracle, or feat of God from the previous devotions encourages you enough to know He can make you invincible in this challenge? (Appendix 5 could help.)

_____

_____

_____

_____

_____

What has God done in your past that encourages you in this challenge?

_____

_____

_____

_____

_____

What encouragement verse used in this devotional encourages you in this challenge? (Use Appendix 7.)

_____

_____

_____

Today's Faith Builder:

What step do you need to take?

_____

_____

_____

Week 5

As followers of Christ, we tend to know that God has taken care of His people. We know of His great feats and His supernatural resources. Unfortunately, we often leave His miraculous interventions in two places: The Old Testament and the life of Jesus. But God's great feats and miracles didn't end there. He didn't limit His victories, provision, and protection in the Old Testament. Jesus didn't stop working with His followers at the Ascension. God continues making His people invincible beyond the ancient days of the Bible, and beyond the Old Testament. He does it today, for you and me.

Provision Given Beyond the Old Testament

From Matthew 17
The Account of God Providing for Taxes

The Challenge Beyond the Old Testament

Some scriptural accounts we've used come from the New Testament, but those are mostly the miracles of Jesus during His earthly ministry. The majority of the accounts come from the Old Testament. There are numerous examples of God's supernatural, life-intervening acts. This is true for the first Christians as well. They saw God's unseen hand at work as they were made invincible. We read about this in the book of Acts. And God continues to work on behalf of his people, even today.

In writing *Invincible*, we hoped to show God's power, while also showing how God cares for and takes interest in us. The second half of that statement may be the most difficult for us to accept.

We more easily accept that God is able to do anything He chooses, but it's harder to believe that He would choose to do something for us, individually. Matthew 10:29–31 gives us the comforting knowledge that God cares about the details of our lives.

Are not two sparrows sold for a penny? And not one of them will fall to the ground apart from your Father. But even the hairs of your head are all numbered. Fear not, therefore; you are of more value than many sparrows (Matthew 10:29–31, ESV).

This is true even in areas of life we may not expect, such as the example in Matthew 17. In the passage, we find Peter being confronted by tax collectors. According to them, both Jesus and Peter's taxes were due. Something with which we all can well relate. Ironically, Jesus and Peter discuss taxes—a common topic of discussion still today.

The need to pay the tax seemed a conundrum for Peter. He had to pay this tax, but due to His commitment to following Jesus, he had left his career—the family fishing business. Peter didn't have a way to earn money and was left without funds to pay his taxes. He was doing the right thing, but the right thing left him without the needed money.

Jesus was also in this same predicament, but Scripture shows He wasn't too worried.

Peter, on the other hand, was worried over this conundrum.

The Provision Beyond the Old Testament

Just as Jesus told the disciples and others at the Sermon on the Mount, our Heavenly Father knows our needs. The Lord knows we have basic necessities to live—food, water, clothing, shelter, and I guess—taxes.

In the passage of Matthew 6, Jesus said God would meet their needs, but that was only if they sought first His kingdom. This wasn't an exchange for needs, but rather a principle of surrender. If we're surrendered to God, we don't have to worry over our needs. He knows what they are, and He will provide.

This was the case with Peter's taxes.

Jesus told him to "go fishing." He told Peter that he'd catch a fish and that first fish would have a coin in its mouth that would pay for the taxes.

So, Peter went fishing.

He caught a fish with a coin in it.

The taxes were provided for, supernaturally.

God cared about the details of Peter's life.

God took care of it.

This was not the Old Testament.

This was in the Gospels and tells how Jesus specifically provided for one of His followers. Jesus still does the same for His followers today. He specifically provides for our needs.

The Lord will take care of us when we surrender our lives to Him.

With the imagery of being a sheep led by a shepherd, King David wrote in the famous Psalm 23: **Surely Your goodness and love will follow me all the days of my life, and I will dwell in the house of the Lord forever (Psalm 23:6, NIV).**

Today's Faith Builder:

Peter brought the problem of the need to pay taxes to Jesus. Take your challenge to Him.

DAY 30
Victory Given Beyond the Old Testament

From Acts
The Account of God Protecting and Empowering the First
Christians

The Challenge Beyond the Old Testament

For the first followers of Christ, as recorded in Acts, they faced a double-edged challenge which would become a double-edged victory.

The first challenge was one given by Jesus. Recorded in Matthew 28:18–20, we call it the Great Commission. From the first disciples to followers of Christ today, our calling is to go into the world and make disciples. It's a mission to spread the Gospel.

More plainly for the Twelve Apostles, it was spelled out in the first chapter of Acts. Acts 1:8 records Jesus telling the disciples before His ascension that they would be His witnesses in Jerusalem, Judea, Samaria, and to the ends of the earth. That's a huge task for the Twelve. It was still a large task for the few thousand of the early church. How would they do this? How would they spread the Gospel? How would they be witnesses in the neighboring regions, much less to the ends of the earth?

That was challenge one.

Challenge two began with the stoning of Stephen. Intense persecution broke out against Christians. First, the persecution came from Jewish leadership in Jerusalem seeking to control what appeared to be a rogue sect of Judaism. The purpose of this persecution was an attempt to extinguish the early church. It was strongest in Jerusalem and Judea.

Persecution continued to rise throughout the first century from Jewish leadership to the Romans.

Followers of Christ were called to be witnesses and to spread the Gospel, but they were being imprisoned and killed for their beliefs.

A double-edged challenge.

How would they find victory?

How would they resemble an invincible army of the Invincible God?

The Victory Beyond the Old Testament

Enemies of Jesus and His followers thought they were winning, but as always, God got the victory.

Two challenges.

The persecution didn't squelch the spreading of the Gospel. Rather, it propelled it.

Luke recorded this history in Acts 8:1, "...On that day a great persecution broke out against the church in Jerusalem, and all except the apostles were scattered throughout Judea and Samaria."

This persecution was terrible, but did you catch where they went?

They'd been in Jerusalem spreading the Gospel. They'd been witnesses in Jerusalem.

First stop in the Acts 1:8 plan.

Next, Jewish leadership persecution pushed them to Judea and Samaria.

Second stop in the Acts 1:8 plan.

And what happened?

Luke saw the triumph in this apparent horrific problem as he wrote in Acts 8:4, "Those who had been scattered preached the Word wherever they went."

Mission accomplished. Challenges shattered. Victory to the Lord. Victory to His people.

When they seemed to be in an impossible situation, by the grace of God, they became invincible.

In Acts 13, Paul and Barnabas launch out to take the Gospel beyond the Levant. The Gospel would be shared, and the number of believers would increase. In these places, the Roman Empire cracked down and the persecution of believers pushed Christ-followers to the ends of the earth, and they witnessed wherever they went.

Third stop in the Acts 1:8 plan.

Historians say that the twelve disciples turned the world upside down and set it on fire. These scholars scratch their heads trying to understand how this small group of uneducated men from Galilee managed to do this. How did they and their message survive despite such intense persecution? How did it spread? It was as if Christ-followers and their message became invincible. It was certainly victorious.

This huge task, and huge triumph, echoes back to God's provision of a son to Abraham and Sarah: **Is anything too hard for the Lord? (Genesis 18:14, NIV).**

Today's Faith Builder:

God continues to bring victory through His people—for 2,000 years—and includes whatever task to which you're called. It's important to remember that the Lord's not stopping anytime soon.

DAY 31

Protection Given Beyond the Old Testament

From Acts 20–27
The Account of God Bringing Paul to Rome

The Challenge Beyond the Old Testament

Yesterday's devotion offered an overview of the book of Acts to some degree and told about the early fulfillment of Acts 1:8. In Acts, the first 12 chapters focus on the work of the apostles in Jerusalem, especially that of Peter. From chapter 13 to the conclusion, the focus is on Paul's missionary work which spanned the whole Mediterranean world. He took three journeys of church planting and disciple-making, and an eventful trip to Rome that completed his recorded travels.

We don't know a great deal about Paul's thought process or God's direction to him in these journeys. A few clues are dropped, but not much. One wonders of a master plan. We do get a peek into these dynamics in Acts 16:6–10. Where the Holy Spirit forbid them from going further into Asia, but eventually led them to Philippi and further west through the "Macedonian Call."

It also appears that Paul had a strategy of planting churches in larger cities, and once churches were established, they'd take the Gospel into surrounding cities in the region. This is especially expressed in the Ephesus work. From Ephesus, mission efforts reached cities like Colossae and Laodicea, along with others. Ephesus was one of the major cities of the Roman Empire. According to Paul's strategy, it's logical to reason that Paul targeted Rome, the main hub of the world at that time.

Whether or not that strategy was the genesis of his missionary ambition to reach Rome, Paul revealed through his letter to Rome that he longed to minister there.

Rome seemed to be a goal for his missionary endeavors. More likely, it was a call planted deep in his soul, as God often does.

But how would Paul get there?

Who would finance the trip?

How would he have the freedom to do so?

The Protection Beyond the Old Testament

The Lord would provide a way, but certainly not the path anyone, not even the daring Paul, would draw up. His path to Rome was unique; it was an all-expenses-paid trip.

Nearing the end of his third journey, Paul felt the need to return to Jerusalem and trouble awaited him there. The Holy Spirit's prompting was right. Trouble waited, along with his ticket to Rome.

First, Paul was captured and beaten by Jewish authorities. Roman authorities then stepped in and imprisoned him. This led to him being taken before the high priests and the regional Roman officials.

Paul was flogged by the Romans but was spared because of his Roman citizenship. Next, a mob tried to kill him, but their plan failed. This resulted in Paul being escorted to prison in Caesarea guarded by 200 soldiers, 70 horsemen, and 200 spearmen. After two years of prison there, the Romans threatened to send him back to the Jewish courts. Paul bypassed the threat by using his Roman citizenship to appeal to Caesar.

Paul was then boarded on a ship in chains—to Rome. That ship faced a dangerous storm, was shipwrecked, and then washed up on an island. On the island, Paul was bitten by a viper, but somehow survived. And finally, he reached Rome, escorted and still under arrest.

He made it.

Mission accomplished.

All along the way, the Holy Spirit kept encouraging Paul, reassuring him that he would reach Rome and stand before the emperor.

Paul appears to experience the worst kind of luck—at least viewed through earthly eyes.

But was it?

In some strange way, Paul managed to complete that journey unscathed. He was invincible. The protection over him, and those with him, was uncanny.

He accomplished the mission. He went to Rome and ministered there. And once that mission was accomplished, he was beheaded.

But until the mission was done, until he went to Rome, he was invincible. And even after that tragic end, He awoke in the presence of the Lord to start eternity.

The difficult path and supernatural protection of Paul on his mission to Rome echo the words of the Psalmist: **Many are** saying of me, "God will not deliver him." But you, Lord, are a shield around me, my glory, the One who lifts my head high (Psalm 3:2–3, NIV). Others around you may not be the only ones feeling that way about your life. You might even feel that way, but God is at work.

Today's Faith Builder:

Take a deep breath today and trust God with the journey. He'll get you where you need to be.

DAY 32
Protection Given Beyond the Bible

From History
The Account of God Protecting Polycarp from Flames

The Challenge Beyond the Bible

The life of second-century Christian, Polycarp, is the perfect place to begin to look at God's continual protection and extending of invincibility into the lives of Christ-followers past the record of Scripture; for his life is a bridge in of itself. Polycarp came to Christ through the teachings of the apostles and was taught by the apostle John. At the end of his life, he was possibly the last Christian to have met one of the Twelve. John was the longest living of the Twelve, and Polycarp lived to be 86. It's also the perfect place to begin because Polycarp's life displays an Old Testament-type miracle, happening at least 65 years from the close of the New Testament.

The account here is indebted to the translations and modernizations of *The Martyrdom of Polycarp,* which was originally written in 160 A.D. and has been provided by the Christian History Institute.[1]

In 155 A.D., Polycarp was a wanted man. He was the Bishop of Smyrna and there was great persecution in the city. No one was a bigger target than the Bishop and his legendary ties to the apostle John. Knowing he was being sought, Polycarp left his home. However, two young men of his household were tortured into confessing his whereabouts. In the evening, the officials followed one of the young men to the home where Polycarp was hiding. Word had made it to him that they were coming in time for him to escape, but he refused saying, "God's will be done."

When the capturers arrived, Polycarp got up from a nap and had dinner prepared for them. After eating, they brought him to the city. Soon, he was brought to the arena and given the chance to recant his faith. Polycarp responded, "Eighty-six years I have served Him [Christ] and He had done me no wrong. How can I blaspheme my King and my Savior?"

Then Polycarp was threatened with having the wild animals let loose on him and he responded, "Call them. It is unthinkable for me to repent from what is good to turn to what is evil. I will be glad though to be changed from evil to righteousness." After the beasts failed to scare him, he was threatened with being burned, to which he replied, "You threaten me with fire which burns for an hour and is then extinguished, but you know nothing of the fire of the coming

---

[1] Graves, Dan, Stephen Tomkins, and J.B. Lightfoot. n.d. "Polycarp's Martyrdom." *Chrisitan History Institute.* Accessed July 19, 2019. https://christianhistoryinstitute.org/study/module/polycarp/.

judgment and eternal punishment, reserved for the ungodly. Why are you waiting? Bring on whatever you want."

Quickly, wood was gathered by the large crowd that chanted, "Down with the atheist!" (This referred to Polycarp because he didn't believe in the Roman deities.)

The Proconsul sought to nail him to the stake, but Polycarp asked not to be nailed. He said, "Leave me as I am, for He that gives me strength to endure the fire, will enable me not to struggle, without the help of your nails."

His hands were tied, and he was made to stand on the wood. The fire was lit. The full arena watched.

The Protection Beyond the Bible

The crowd watched and to their surprise, Polycarp wasn't burned. Supernaturally, the flames formed an arch, like a wind-filled ship sail, all the way around his body. The fire didn't touch him. Also, the air was filled with a sweet scent like from precious spices.

Polycarp wasn't burning. He was being supernaturally protected. He was invincible.

But the physical protection was short-lived. He was run through by a sword.

Yet, his death wasn't in vain. Spectators recalled the stark difference in behavior between the followers of Christ and the lost. Polycarp displayed such faith, while the capturers, those who gathered wood, those who cursed him, and the one who killed him proved the existence of evil in their hearts.

Though his life was taken, and his enemies seemed to have triumphed in that day, his foes were shown for who they were. The power of Christ was glorified. Such a vindication is reminiscent of what David said about the victories God had given him. **When the wicked advance against me to devour me, it is my enemies and my foes who will stumble and fall (Psalm 27:2, NIV).**

Today's Faith Builder:

Even in your proverbial capture, you can still display faith. Commit never to recant your faith.

DAY 33
Provision Given Beyond the Bible

From History
The Account of God Providing for George Mueller

The Challenge Beyond the Bible

For this example of God providing beyond the Bible, we advance over 1,600 years to the mid-1800s in Bristol, England to the life of George Mueller. A man who'd likely top the Hall of Faith of Hebrews 11, if there was a second edition to Hebrews.

Today's devotion uses multiple articles that are cited, including John Piper's 2004 presentation on Mueller.[2]

Growing up in modern-day Germany, Mueller was far from the example he set in his later years as a teenager and young adult.

> *By sixteen he was a liar, a thief, a swindler, a drunkard, and in jail. Yet, God worked in the young man's soul and brought him to Himself...He left behind the profligacy and self-seeking of his old life and became totally devoted*

---

[2] Piper, John. 2004. "George Mueller's Strategy for Showing God: Simplicity of Faith, Sacred Scripture, and Satisfaction in God." *Desiring God.* February 3. Accessed July 20, 2019. https://www.desiringgod.org/messages/george-muellers-strategy-for-showing-god#11.

to serving his Lord. Humility came to mark Mueller's life, for he depended on God for everything, viewing himself as a tool in the hands of the Master Workman.[3]

Though Mueller would recount his sinful life as that young man, his life proved God had made a radical change. He originally set off to London to be trained to be a missionary but became sick. An unnamed man restored him and forever changed his view of ministry. His passion for the Lord rubbed hard against the complacency of the day. He became disillusioned with the faithless doctrines of the day and the worldly strategies used by Christian agencies, particularly the strategy of going into debt. This led to him found a ministry.

Mueller's ministry had a five-fold plan. First, create schools for children and adults to teach Bible knowledge. Second, distribute Bibles. Third, provide support to missionaries. Fourth, distribute tracts and books. Fifth, board, clothe, and scripturally educate destitute children whose parents had died. He dreamed these things on no small scale. His son-in-law would say, "He devised large and liberal things for the Lord's cause."[4] The fifth branch of the strategy included creating orphanages.

These things were large in and of themselves, but Mueller was also convicted that none of these things should be done by going into debt or taking loans. He believed that this

---

[3] Christianity.com. n.d. "George Mueller, Man of Faith and Prayer." *Christianity.com.* Accessed July 20, 2019. https://www.christianity.com/church/church-history/timeline/1801-1900/george-mueller-man-of-faith-and-prayer-11630420.html.

[4] George Mueller, A Narrative of Some of the Lord's Dealing with George Muller, Written by Himself, Jehovah Magnified. Addresses by George Muller Complete and Unabridged, 2 vols. (Muskegon, Mich.: Dust and Ashes, 2003), 264.

extended to his own salary and survival. For his salary and his ministry endeavors, he never solicited funds, but only through faithfully praying did he receive unsolicited funds. This wasn't just a preferable method, but a deep calling within him.

Through his own words, he gave the reasons for this operation by faith.

- *The orphan houses exist to display that God can be trusted and to encourage believers to take Him at His Word.*
- His passion was: *to display with open proofs that God could be trusted with the practical affairs of life.*
- His aim was: *live a life and lead a ministry in a way that proves God is real, God is trustworthy, and God answers prayer.*
- Often, he wrote that he wanted to increase others' confidence in God.

The endeavors of his work were challenging enough, but to do so without asking for a cent added another layer of difficulty.

Would God come through?

Would these plans succeed?

The Provision Beyond the Bible

Yes, God came through.

Yes, the plans succeeded.

Mueller's schools and orphanages grew to such massive levels that they completely transformed England.

And all was done without soliciting funds. Nor did Mueller ever take a salary.

His journal reveals close calls and last-minute provisions, but most magnificently his journal recalls over 10,000 answered prayers.

Mueller accomplished his mission and more. Today, people still have an increased confidence in God because of him.

In a presentation on Mueller, Piper said,

> *The accomplishments of all five branches were significant, but the one he was known for around the world in his own lifetime, and still today, was the orphan ministry. He built five large orphan houses and cared for 10,024 orphans in his life. When he started in 1834, there were accommodations for 3,600 orphans in all of England, and twice that many children under eight were in prison. One of the great effects of Mueller's ministry was to inspire others so that "fifty years after Mr. Mueller began his work, at least one hundred thousand orphans were cared for in England alone."[5]*

The restriction that Mueller put on his life and ministry to not ask for funds would appear to be a hindrance, but it certainly wasn't. In his lifetime, an estimated 8 million dollars

---

[5] Piper, John. 2004.

passed through his hands, none of which was for his own life. Mueller had $800 dollars to his name when he died.[6]

Mueller's life is an incredible example of provision from God. Like Elijah on Mount Carmel, he dared to ask God to prove Himself mighty and God gladly did. This shows that God still provides and still makes his people invincible. All Mueller did was ask and God provided. It brings to mind what King David experienced time after time and wrote in the Psalms: **I called to the LORD, who is worthy of praise, and I have been saved from my enemies (Psalm 18:3, NIV).**

Today's Faith Builder:

Do as Mueller did in his prayer journals—ask the Lord for what you need.

---

[6] Eisenbart, David A. 2012. *In Search of God: Decoding Reality.* Xulon Press, 64.

Victory Given Beyond the Bible

From Modern History
The Account of God Saving the Waodani Tribe

The Challenge Beyond the Bible

The account retold in today's devotion takes us further into modern history. The central event of this account occurred in 1956, but the work still continues today. It gives us a fuller understanding of what it means to say that we're invincible and provides a better view of God giving victory even when it appears as if we're failing.

The account here is taken from multiple articles that are cited, as the events have been well documented.

In 1950, a former Ecuadorean missionary told a 23-year-old ministry student at Wheaton College about an uncivilized, ruthless, and unreached tribe in the jungle of Ecuador known as the Waodani. That moment was a catalyst for Jim Elliot to become a missionary to those people. By early 1952, Jim was headed to Ecuador with his missionary partner, Pete Fleming. Eventually, Jim and his wife, Elisabeth, became part of a missionary team working to reach this tribe. Three years later, they made contact with the Waodani.

They knew the Waodani were extremely dangerous. Yet, they felt a calling to reach this group.

What a task. American missionaries sent to learn the language and the culture, then travel into the jungle to reach a tribe of uncivilized warriors.

As with so many callings and missions given by God in the Old Testament, New Testament, and the 1,900 years before these missionaries, it seemed daunting. Yet, they knew God's promise of protection and provision. He was the One that would bring victory. If truly called to this mission, then they would be invincible until completion.

The Victory Beyond the Bible

All appeared to be going to plan. Missionary pilot, Nate Saint, developed a method to give gifts to the tribe. For months, the missionaries would use this method. They'd also use loudspeakers to proclaim peaceful greetings. Eventually, the Waodani reciprocated and the team felt it was time to make contact.

A beach along a river in the jungle was used as a landing strip, and on January 2, 1956, one by one, the team of the five missionaries were flown into the jungle. Jim Elliot, Pete Fleming, Ed McCully, Nate Saint, and Roger Youderian made initial positive contact with the tribe, but a few days later, the contact turned tragic. All five missionaries were speared and left dead on that beach.

Shockwaves of this failed missionary attempt ran through the United States.

Young wives were left widowed.

Young children were left fatherless.

A tribe was left unreached.

So much for victory. So much for protection. So much for invincibility.

But the story wasn't over, and what shouldn't be a shocker to us, was that God was at work the whole time.

Two years later, Elisabeth, the widow of Jim, along with their three-year-old daughter and Nate's sister, made contact with the Waodani and went to live with them. Elisabeth lived with the tribe for five years. During that time, many of them came to follow Christ.

Nate's son, Steve, stayed summers among the tribe as a boy. Nine years after the death of his father and the others, Steve was baptized by two of the tribesmen who had killed his father. His baptism was in the river that ran along the beach where those missionaries died. Steve continues to work with the Waodani to this day.

Through temporal eyes and worldly wisdom, this tale doesn't make much sense. But from eternal eyes, it tells the story of how God and His people will be victorious and are invincible.

Yes, Jim and the other four died, but they walked straight into glory. They were promoted to an even better life.

The mission was accomplished. An unreached people became reached. Brutal murderers became faithful saints.

Even beyond reaching this Ecuadorean tribe, Jim's main passion was that more people would become missionaries. According to one article regarding Jim, "In his death...he probably inspired more people to go to other countries to share the love of Jesus than he ever could have in life."[7]

This is the invincibility of the follower of Christ.

Elliot defined our invincibility the best, when he said, "He is no fool who gives what he cannot keep to gain that which he cannot lose."

The apostle Paul wrote something very similar: **It is my eager expectation and hope that I will not be at all ashamed, but that with full courage now, as always, Christ will be honored in my body, whether by life or by death. For to me to live is Christ, and to die is gain (Philippians 1:20–21, ESV).**

Today's Faith Builder:

Remember we only see a small portion of the plan of the now. God is at work on the full plan.

---

[7] (Christianity.com n.d.)

Invincibility Given to You Beyond the Bible

From Current Events
The Account of God Working in the World Today

The Challenge Now

As noted in the last few devotions, God is still at work just as He was in the Old Testament, the life of Christ, and the New Testament. In the same vein, He's calling His people and assigning missions just as He did in the past. It continues with you and me. We're all called. We're called to faithfully follow Him, and we're called to make disciples. And if you follow Him long enough, you'll be given specific assignments. Nothing has changed in God's involvement of His people in His plans.

The challenges of walking faithfully and carrying out the Great Commission haven't faded either. It may even be a correct assessment to say the challenges have ramped up. As bad as persecution was in the first century, a glimpse of which you see in the earlier devotional of the martyrdom of Polycarp, it's even worse now. In developed nations like the United States, the temptations and challenges upon one's faithful walk have greatly increased with the development and use of technology, the increase in immorality, and the distractions we add to our lives.

It's a tough battle. It's tough to stay the course. Life can hit us with so much.

Then, to add the assignment of the Great Commission—it's tough. And, if we're honest, doubt erodes our belief that God works in us as He did in the past.

Does He?

The Invincibility Given Now

Author and missionary, Tom Doyle, through his works published by Thomas Nelson, is doing the best work showing the world that God is still at work today like in the record of Scripture.

His books to date:

- *Dreams and Visions*[8]—Tells real accounts of Jesus appearing to Muslims in the Middle East in dreams or visions leading to their salvation. The stories weave elements of God working in miraculous ways on many fronts.
- *Killing Christians*[9]—Tells real accounts of Christians who've remained faithful even when facing fierce persecution. The stories show the strength God gives.
- *Standing in the Fire*[10]—Tells real accounts of Christians remaining faithful in dangerous situations. These stories show God giving

---

[8] Doyle, T., & Webster, G. (2012). *Dreams and Visions*. Nashville: W Publishing Group.

[9] Doyle, T., & Webster, G. (2015). *Killing Christians*. Nashville: W Publishing Group.

[10] Doyle, T., & Webster, G. (2017). *Standing in the Fire*. Nashville: W Publishing Group.

miraculous victories, provision, and protection to His people.

I encourage you, when you finish this devotional book, pick up Doyle's books and read just one story per day as a devotional. It's powerful.

With so many stories from his works, it's impossible to do any of them justice in this restricted space, but the most impactful for me is found in *Standing in the Fire*. Chapter 5, "Just the Usual Damascus Death Threat" tells of the Gospel impacting the Druze. The Druze are a people group located in Syria, Lebanon, Israel, and Jordan. Their religion is unique, and its roots trace back to Moses' father-in-law, Jethro. At least in Syria prior to the account Doyle gives, none had become Christians.

A young man, Kareem, felt called by God to move his family and live among the Druze people in Syria. On multiple layers, this was dangerous. For one, Syria was still in the height of its conflict. In addition, to share the Gospel with the Druze could cost him his life.

After a year of praying and trying to share, Kareem and his family made zero converts. He had managed to receive multiple threats and made numerous trips to the police station. Convinced the mission was failing, he and his wife began considering a move back home.

Then, one day out of the blue, a Druze father showed up at Kareem's front door. The man was distraught. His daughter had cancer and doctors hadn't given her long to live. They'd tried everything. All they could think to do was ask this Christian family to pray for their daughter. Kareem did. Never having seen a miraculous healing himself, he was reluctant.

165

By simply offering that prayer, Kareem was arrested and beaten severely. He was released but had been worked over. A week passed. No converts. No progress. The only gain was the pain that lingered from the beating. Then something happened— a knock on the door.

They opened the door, braced and expecting to see the police, but instead, over 50 Druze people stood there in line. All had heard that the young girl this Christian prayed healing over had been healed. They, too, were coming to receive prayers for healing. The young girl was now cancer free and doctors could not explain it.

Many were healed, and it was only the start of many more miracles. Even more importantly, Druze people came to Jesus, and they still are.

Tom wrote about this in 2017. It's very recent.

God is still at work—still calling us to dangerous missions and making us invincible in them.

This is the world we live in.

This is the world in which you're to follow Christ and know you're invincible. You could be a Kareem.

Jesus was clear in the calling of the disciples, and therefore us, that the road would not be easy. He was also clear that through Him we could come out the victor: "...**In this world you will have trouble. But take heart! I have overcome the world**" (John 16:33, NIV).

Today's Faith Builder:
Ask yourself if you're in the story God is telling today.

Week 6

IN THE END

Every day, believers are challenged in their faith, and their mission is difficult. Scripture also tells of a time when the challenges will be even greater. This time is at the end of the age. God promises to be with His people even then. He promises to bring them through unshaken. This time of the end is also when we will see the greatest displays of victory, provision, and protection of God's people. Whether we will be in that generation or not, we need to know we're invincible—now, at the end of the age, and into the age to come.

DAY 36

God Preserves His People in the End

From Revelation 12
The Account of God Keeping His Promise to Preserve Israel

The Challenge in the End

I just had a conversation with my daughter. We postponed a trip to the waterpark so I could finish this book. Technically, I didn't make a promise, but I did change plans. I backed myself into a corner with the plans I originally made and was unable to keep. I'm careful in the plans I make because I know I can't always keep them.

Have you ever considered that God has backed Himself into a huge corner with His countless and detailed promises? In fact, He's staked His reputation and even the proof of His existence on coming through 100%. That's one corner of which I'd never get out. I can't control situations, I'm at the mercy of them.

But God's not at the mercy of anything.

God, at the mercy of nothing, has kept all His promises for the nearly 6,000 years of human history. And there are still promises on the table. The majority of the remaining promises will be put to the test at the end of the age. Some of His major

169

promises that will be ultimately fulfilled in the end have already been greatly tested many times in history.

Most of them center on preserving the descendants of Abraham—the Jews. These promises began with Abraham and are first told in Genesis 12 and 15. From that time, it was promised that the nation would continue, that they'd become numerous, that they'd have the land which is modern-day Israel, and they'd be a blessing to all other nations. This promise was also given to Abraham's son, Isaac, then Isaac's son, Jacob, and then to all of Jacob's sons. A covenant was made. It was an unconditional covenant, meaning God would bring it to pass no matter what Abraham's descendants did. This Abrahamic Covenant is intended to stand for eternity.

More was added to the promise in 2 Samuel 7, when God promised there'd be a Son of David who would rule from Jerusalem for eternity. This Davidic Covenant also was unconditional and is to stand for eternity.

More promises came through the prophets, who warned Israel would be removed from the land and punished because of idolatry and sin. But sometime, they'd be brought back to the land and restored, and all the promises to Abraham and David would be fulfilled.

The New Testament also added details, that even though many Jews rejected Jesus as the Messiah and hardened their hearts towards God, God would still restore them. He'd not just restore the land, but also restore them spiritually.

These are daunting promises—an impossible challenge for anyone to keep.

Then consider the adversary who has always targeted God's people. Revelation 12 reveals that his main target throughout history and in the last days is Israel—the Jews.

Everything in this world is working against the fulfillment of God's promises to Israel.

The Protection in the End

Though the challenges may appear impossible to us, they are not for God. He cuts through the challenges like a hot knife in butter.

He's already thwarted plans of Satan working through human agents to foil the preservation of the Jews.

- When famine and drought threatened to wipe them out, God sent Joseph ahead into Egypt to provide food for Israel.
- When the Egyptians tried to kill all the Israelite babies, God didn't allow it.
- When the Egyptians tried to keep them enslaved, God delivered them.
- When the Egyptian army tried to destroy them, God swallowed Pharaoh's army into the Red Sea.
- When the Assyrians sought to conquer not just Israel, but also Judah, an angel killed 185,000 soldiers in one night.
- When the Babylonians tried to keep them captive, God had Cyrus overtake them.

171

- When Haman and the Persians sought to kill them all, God had placed Esther in a place for a time such as this.
- When the Romans destroyed Jerusalem and dispersed Jews around the world, the Jews were still preserved.
- When Hitler's final solution sought to wipe Jews from the globe, it was stopped.
- Now God has brought Jews back into the land.
- God has given them their own nation.
- God has given Jerusalem back to them.

God has kept His promises.

Scripture tells us there are still more challenges ahead. Anti-Semitism is growing in the world and is higher than at the time of the Holocaust. The world seems determined to carve land away from Israel. Many Jews still haven't accepted Jesus.

Prophecy also tells us the time of Jacob's trouble is on the horizon. This is a time when Israel will face greater difficulties than ever before.

But prophecy also speaks of a remnant being protected and eventually coming back to Christ. It also says the promised Son of David, Jesus, will come and defeat Israel's enemies and establish an eternal kingdom.

History has shown that God is sure to complete the fulfillment of these prophecies. A saying traced back to the physician of the Prussian King, Frederick the Great, is that the greatest proof of the existence of God is the Jews. Modern apologists have repeated this statement. They recognize that the national historic peers of Israel in the Bible are no more, yet Israel remains.

This truth of God will be made manifest even more greatly in the end and brings to mind a statement in the book of Jude. He was speaking on how the Lord can keep us from stumbling in our faith, but the phrase "keep us" is more than relevant for God's protection. **To Him who is able to keep you from stumbling and to present you before His glorious presence without fault and with great joy (Jude 1:24, NIV).**

David expressed his experience, as well as God's relationship and protection of Israel, in Psalm 17: **Keep me as the apple of Your eye; hide me in the shadow of Your wings from the wicked who are out to destroy me, from my mortal enemies who surround me (Psalm 17:8–9, NIV).**

Today's Faith Builder:

Reflect on God's preservation of a people for over 4,500 years. Surely, He can keep you.

DAY 34
Jesus is the Victor in the End

From Revelation 19
The Account of Jesus Defeating the Antichrist

The Challenge in the End

There's been a strict goal of making sure each devotional is aimed at how we—you and I, and all followers of Christ—are the ones who are invincible and will win. Certainly, it's only through Christ that we are invincible, but often we don't see how He has and will impart that to us. For the next three devotionals, we're going to change things up. We'll be looking at Jesus as the Invincible One and the Victor. We need to see that, in the midst of the worst times we will ever experience on earth, though it may seem like His people and His cause is losing, Jesus will be the Victor, the Champion. By following Him *now*, we'll be on His side *then*, and we'll be fellow partakers of that victory.

As stated throughout this devotional, there are daily struggles for the cause of Christ and His people. We've not seen anything yet. The full onslaught against the Lord will happen at the end of this age when we hit the final three-and-a-half-year countdown.

Daniel 9 tells of a final, seven years of this age. It'll begin with the Antichrist rising to power and making a covenant of

175

peace with Israel. For three and a half years, he'll uphold it. There will be peace, at least in the Holy Land, but likely wars around the globe. Jews in Israel will be protected, but the same probably can't be said for Christians around the world. The international church will look like a rag-tag army. Many will have turned away. We'll have turned against each other as we see in Matthew 24.

Then, at the midpoint of those final seven years, the Antichrist will commit what's called the abomination of desolation. He'll set himself (or an image of himself) up to be worshipped in the temple. Then he'll turn against the Jews. Intense persecution will be waged against them. Some will escape into the wilderness, but Scripture warns many will fall.

This will rage on for some time as we read in Revelation 12.

The Antichrist will then draw the armies of the world to Israel to wipe God's people off the map. It will look bleak.

This time will be the most desperate in the history of Israel.

In the same way Jerusalem was surrounded by the Assyrians, Babylonians, Romans, and Turks, the armies of the world will be breathing down Israel's neck.

The Victory in the End

Scripture describes that, in the last second, the heavens will open up and there will be One on a White Horse. Scripture says He'll be the One called Faithful and True. His eyes will be like a blazing fire. He'll wear many crowns. His robe will be dipped in blood. Out of His mouth will come a sharp sword. On His thighs

176

will be written: King of Kings and Lord of Lords. Following Him will be the Army of Heaven, a mix of angels and us—those who have been born again and at that point have been raptured/resurrected to Him.

This is Jesus.

He's returned.

He's clearly visible as the Messiah.

He's clearly invincible.

He's clearly the Victor.

This is the account from Revelation 19.

Scripture gives more detail of Jesus' return, expressing that there could be a procession, possibly from Sinai or even Egypt up to Jerusalem. We're simplifying the return here focusing on the aspect of the victory over the Antichrist.

But think about this: Jesus will return.

And when He does, He comes against the Antichrist, the false prophet, the kings, the commanders, and all who are gathered against God's people. It sounds like the Army of Heaven, us, gets a front-row seat of Jesus annihilating the enemy and saving His people. The victory will be so decisive, it's described as Jesus trampling grapes in a winepress. In Revelation 14, the apostle John writes that the flow of blood from the Antichrist's coalition will be to the height of a horse's bridle and will extend for 180 miles. In Revelation 19, the victory is described as so dominant that *all* birds of the air would have flesh of the Antichrist's army to feed upon.

Then as Scripture proclaims, every knee on Earth will bow to Jesus.

He wins.

He's invincible.

He's the Victor.

This is the One who Matthew 28:30 says is with us right now.

He's not one to mess with. Our enemies need to be on notice. Our struggles need to be warned. This conquering Jesus is the One we follow.

Paul often told believers to look for Jesus' coming—it was the instruction he gave both Timothy and Titus. He told Titus: **We wait for the blessed hope—the appearing of the glory of our great God and Savior, Jesus Christ (Titus 2:13, NIV).**

Today's Faith Builder:

Commit to staying on His side. He is our hope. He is our Savior.

DAY 38

Jesus is the King in the End

From Revelation 20
The Account of Jesus Ruling in the Millennial Kingdom

The Challenge in the End

In Day 36, you read about the promises God made to Israel through Abraham and later, David. In 2 Samuel 7, a promise was given that would serve as an underlying theme throughout the rest of Scripture and history. David, and therefore his kingdom, Israel, was promised that a descendant of his would sit on the throne in Jerusalem and rule all the nations of the world for eternity.

Israel looked for that fulfillment with Solomon, but God had a plan to unfold. We already know who the descendant of David was who fulfilled the plan. Jesus. He was the Anointed One. Messiah. Christ. The promised King of the Jews.

Through His first coming, participation in this kingdom was expanded to Gentiles. Gentiles were adopted into Jesus' Jewish family.

Now we are waiting as the rest of God's plan unfolds.

Not only do we know that it is, indeed, unfolding before our very eyes, we also know how it comes to fruition. When Jesus returns, He'll defeat the Antichrist and his army. Revelation 20 reveals more of what will happen at that time. Satan will be locked up in the abyss. Jesus will rule physically—in person—from Jerusalem. His kingdom, initially torn with war and tribulation, will begin to rebuild. Finally, long-awaited peace will be brought upon the whole world in the Millennial Kingdom.

According to Scripture, nations will still exist, but Jerusalem will be the capital of the world.

There will be survivors from the previous age, and they will live their lives, marrying and having children. Life expectancies will be longer. It'll be a true utopia, far better than any mankind could ever dream of creating.

We'll be there. Remember from yesterday, when Jesus returns, we'll follow Him. We'll have perfect, glorified bodies like He had after the resurrection. We'll be immortal. Scripture says we'll rule with Him.

Though these descriptions of the Millennial Kingdom may be difficult to grasp, it's what a straight-forward reading of Scripture presents.

The bottom line is that Jesus is back on Earth. We're with Him.

And most importantly, He's King.

Jesus is King.

What a coronation that will be!

Things will rock on wonderfully for a thousand years.

Then, according to God's plan, Satan is let loose. And one more time, he repeats the pattern that ended the previous age. He'll deceive many. He'll start a rebellion against Jesus. He'll march against Jerusalem. His large army will surround Jesus' capital.

The Victory in the End

It's impossible to build suspense as we tell the story.

We already know who Jesus is and what He is capable of doing.

Jesus again will squelch the rebellion.

He'll again completely conquer.

He'll again annihilate the enemy.

This time, though, Satan will be thrown into the lake of fire.

Again, there will be a showdown.

Again, Jesus will win.

Is there any doubt as to which team we should be on?

These victories and the sentencing of His enemies are why Jesus' words to John the Apostle on the Isle of Patmos should comfort us: **"Do not be afraid. I am the First and the Last. I am the Living One; I was dead, and now look, I am alive for ever and ever! And I hold the keys of death and Hades (Revelation 1:17–18, NIV).**

Today's Faith Builder:

Doubly commit to staying on His side. Take comfort that Jesus, your King, is and always will be victorious.

DAY 30

God is with His People in the End

From Revelation 21
The Account of God Dwelling with His People Again

The Challenge Throughout the Ages

Following Creation when the earth was brand new, Adam and Eve had it made.

They were perfect and without sin.

The Garden was perfect with no curse.

The unseen world blurred into the seen world.

And most of all, God the Father, dwelt with them. He walked with them in the cool of the day.

They talked to Him directly.

But then, came their disobedience.

Their rebellion.

Their sin ended that perfect scenario.

They were no longer without guilt and shame.

They were no longer without sin.

They were kicked out of the Garden.

The earth was cursed.

The unseen world was walled off.

There was also a price mankind had to pay because of their sin—they'd have to face God's wrath.

And worst of all, God the Father, was separated from them. His holiness keeps Him away from sin.

God didn't want for us to be forever separated from Him. Even at the beginning of history, God hinted at a plan to restore all that was lost in the Garden, and especially our relationship with Him. The hints are in the form of the coverings made from animal skins that God made for Adam and Eve. The skins meant that animals had to die. They provide a reminder of the need for a sacrifice of blood as well as the need for a covering from guilt. Finally, in the prophecy of Genesis 3:15, we are given a glimpse of a Savior that would come.

And that Savior has come.

The ultimate sacrifice of blood was made.

Our sins are covered if we trust in Christ.

God's wrath is appeased by Jesus' death on the cross.

This is where we are presently in history. Jesus has come and been that sacrifice. It's up to us to accept it and follow Him by faith.

Then slowly through the Millennial Kingdom, lost aspects of Eden will begin to be restored. Believers will have perfect, sinless bodies like Adam and Eve. Still, aspects of the curses and separation would remain.

Now, the question becomes, will that perfect paradise ever be restored? Will God dwell with His people again?

The Joy in the End

The answer is YES!

After Jesus defeats Satan's final rebellion and throws him into the lake of fire, the earth is made new. Peter writes that it will be refined in fire. However, when the renewal takes place, there will be a New Heaven and New Earth. The entire earth will return to an Edenic state. No more curse. No more sin. No more separation from the unseen world. All restored.

Also, New Jerusalem, this beautiful city with streets of gold and gates made of solid pearl, will come down upon the earth. The city is 1,400 miles long, 1,400 miles wide, and 1,400 miles tall. This is the place prepared for us. We get the best of both worlds—the amazing city and the Edenic Earth. And we get to enjoy it for eternity.

This sounds like the ultimate prize.

But there is more!

As in the Garden of Eden, God the Father will dwell with us.

In Revelation 21:22–23 we read, "I did not see a temple in the city, because the Lord God Almighty and the Lamb are its temple. The city does not need the sun or the moon to shine on it, for the glory of God gives it light, and the Lamb is its lamp."

This is our reward for belonging to Christ.

It's the reward for faithful following. It should be motivation for us to carry out the mission He has given us.

The wonders mentioned in the last two devotionals, the Millennial Kingdom and the New Earth, help explain why Paul could write, "**For our light and momentary troubles are achieving for us an eternal glory that far outweighs them all. So, we fix our eyes not on what is seen, but on what is unseen, since**

what is seen is temporary, but what is unseen is eternal."
(Corinthians 4:17–18, NIV).

Now, God will physically give us supernatural victories, provision, and protection in this age. Chances are, you've already experienced this. Trusting in that possibility gives us the full right to say that through Christ we're invincible. Knowing what lies ahead—the Millennial Kingdom, the New Earth, the New Jerusalem, and dwelling with God the Father for eternity—the reward we will one day receive, helps us keep things in perspective when we face trials, troubles, and even death. Because the truth remains.

In Christ, we're invincible.

If we're threatened with any daily problem—what's the worst that could happen?

If we're threatened with a scary step of faith—what's the worst that could happen?

If we're facing persecution—what's the worst that could happen?

We die?

What then? For followers of Christ, death means life in paradise in the presence of the Lord. It means witnessing Jesus return to Earth in glorious, conquering victory. It means receiving an immortal body and participating in the Millennial Kingdom. And then retiring to an eternity of a Garden-of-Eden Earth and a city that might take just as long to explore.

Yeah, I'd say we're invincible.

Today's Faith Builder:

Lock this picture of the age to come into your mind.

You're Invincible in the End

From Revelation 1
The Account of Jesus Walking with You

Your Challenge in the End

Jesus said that each day has enough trouble of its own. You've probably found that out.

He also said in Matthew 24:21, "For then there will be great distress, unequaled from the beginning of the world until now—and never to be equaled again."

So, we're facing trouble now. And honestly, we're not handling it all that well. Further, at the end of the age, there's going to be trouble the likes of which mankind has never known. That doesn't sound like it's going to be an easy walk in the park. If we are struggling now, how will we handle things when the REAL trouble comes? The answer is Jesus.

We've seen in the last couple of devotions that Jesus makes easy work of those difficult days. He's the first and the last. He was the first One in existence and if He didn't extend an opportunity for us to join Him in eternity, we would be utterly lost. He holds the keys to Hades and death. He's no one to mess with and we're on His side. He also told us in Matthew 28:20 that He would be with us—always. Come what may. This means He is with us now and will be with us "even to the end of the age." He's with us in the daily troubles and He will be with us when it all hits the proverbial fan.

This promise is for you and me.

It's not an idealistic thought, either. It is real and it is true. His presence is with us through the indwelling of the Holy Spirit. All the time, He is with us.

Though we certainly are equipped and empowered, let's not downplay the coming difficulty. Often when Scripture mentions this time of trouble, there are also warnings to not be overcome by fear. There must be frightening times ahead.

The Protection in the End

Fear will come, but we must remember that Jesus is with us.

Around the time of the writing of the book of Revelation, believers were in a time of intense persecution. Christians were drug into arenas, fed to wild animals, and slaughtered for sport. They were burned at stakes. They were hung on poles to be lights for parties. Times were bleak. It was in that context that John the Apostle received the book of Revelation. John himself was facing difficulty. He'd been burned alive in oil but survived. Then, he was exiled to an island by himself. So, the writer of Revelation, its recipients, and the times in which it was written were fraught with great challenges. The content of the book of Revelation also deals with great challenges believers will face.

However, at the beginning of the book of Revelation, Jesus offers hope and comfort. It reminds the reader that from

Jesus we receive grace to stand firm unto the end. And the glorious ending is that He is coming again! Revelation has given encouragement to believers throughout the ages. And it also was meant to encourage those living in the last days.

The time of the writing of the book of Revelation was a pivotal moment in Christianity. Those persecuting followers of Christ were hoping to extinguish the young movement. But, by the grace of God seen through the faithfulness of His followers even unto their deaths, God was glorified, and the movement grew—Jesus was victorious. His victory to come is also described in Revelation 1. The description given of Jesus is much like the one in Revelation 19, when He returns and wins the day. The same sword Jesus has at Armageddon is with Him in the first chapter of Revelation, too.

The appearance of Jesus to John also included Him walking between seven lampstands which represented literal churches. Jesus held, in His right hand, seven stars that represented the leadership in those churches. The imagery is clear and harkens back to the Great Commission when Jesus sent His followers out and said He'd be with them. In the vision, He's in the middle of them, walking alongside them. He's there to protect and provide for them.

This is a picture that encouraged His early followers and it should also encourage us. Jesus is walking in our midst. And He's not the Suffering Servant this time, He's the Warrior Jesus.

Like David walking out to face Goliath in full confidence, Jesus is walking to fight our battles. It was in the context of this vision in which Jesus said, "I am the Alpha and the Omega," says the Lord God, "Who is, and who was, and who is to come, the

Almighty." He also said, "Do not be afraid. I am the First and the Last."

The conclusion of the book of Revelation is much like its opening—Jesus is coming back in victory. John relayed the words of Jesus: "Look, I am coming soon! My reward is with me, and I will give to each person according to what they have done. I am the Alpha and the Omega, the First and the Last, the Beginning and the End" (Revelation 22:12, NIV).

We're invincible because of Jesus in us.

He's promised to be with us to the end.

And there in Revelation, He reaffirms His presence.

It's in this context that the most popular encouragement verse in Scripture should be framed. Paul wrote and we all know, **"I can do all things through Christ who strengthens me" (Philippians 4:13, NKJV).** There is profound meaning in this verse. It applies to our daily lives and in the context of completing the calling God has given each of us.

A calling to faithfully follow Him.

A calling to make disciples.

A calling that may be specifically given.

Whatever it is, you can do it. He is with you and gives you strength.

That strength makes you INVINCIBLE.

Today, Tomorrow, and Everyday After's Faith Builder:

Shout at the top of your lungs—I'm INVINCIBLE through Christ!

192

Write everywhere you will look—I'm INVINCIBLE through Christ!

Shrug off the difficulty, the struggle, the trial, the bad news, the challenge, or whatever that is weighing you down.

Throw off every sin that is entangling.

Step anywhere the Lord has said to step—it's time—for in Christ, you are INVINCIBLE!

Appendix 1

CLARIFICATION

Invincible is a Strong Word and Idea, Did We Overreach?

An Argument

As this devotional book and sermons related to it have been shared, readers and audiences have cringed at the word and idea "invincible." There's agreement that God does give victory. He provides. He protects. He can make the impossible possible. God's protection and provision didn't end with the Bible. He will be the victor in the end. All of this is given a thumbs up and considered true, but invincibility seems like a stretch.

We, too, have struggled with this term. For God's people do seem to lose battles even if the war belongs to them. They do become imprisoned. They do get killed for their faith. They do go without food or possessions. Difficulty does come for the follower of Christ. Is invincible a bit strong and overreaching?

That's a fair question. But is that uneasiness a theology question or a faith issue? We'd argue it's the second. Since the enlightenment and the later counter-act of neo-orthodoxy, the supernatural has been removed from Western Christianity. We tend to be a jaded people in terms of God working miraculously on our behalf, or of Him even crossing into our daily lives.

We may have overreached, but it's not theologically incorrect, rather it's the raising of the bar of faith. It's a call to the faith we need now and will certainly need at the end of the age. Don't brush off the word, invincible, as branding or a cute title. Rather, let that level of faith push you and grow your faith. The belief that you're invincible in Christ is the goal. Remember this 40-day journey was designed to increase your faith muscles. Let invincibility be the poster on the wall. Let it be the goal you're working toward. Then, let it be the reality moving forward to stand firm and march on.

A Definition

Accepting the term, invincible, has been tough for audiences. We get it. We've been asked multiple times to define the invincibility of the believer. We've been reluctant to do so because God teaches us this truth by having us wrestle with how the promises of God mesh with the reality of death, sickness, and hard times that Christians face. Though those realities are true, there's clearly promises in Scripture of victory, provision, protection, and the impossible made possible. These promises from God are the power behind this 40-day devotional. Yet, for fear that the vagueness will lead to confusion, here is a definition. It's buried deep in this section so there's still room for you to wrestle.

The invincibility of the believer is: *When a follower of Christ follows in obedience to the mission given through the Holy Spirit and the Word of God, the believer can trust with certainty that the mission will be accomplished to the Lord's desired results, and that even the worst that could possibly happen to them, a*

196

physical death, is merely a promotion into paradise. The mission given and glorification of God will happen, and all the provision and protection a believer needs in the process will be provided according to the eternal wisdom of God taking into account the big picture of our lives, His will, and the ultimate good.

Appendix 2

CALLING & MISSION

What is it that You've Been Called to Do?

Throughout these devotions, references are constantly made to the calling or mission God has given you. This distinction is important because the invincibility imparted to you is promised for the calling or mission you've been given. God will give victory, provision, and protection while you're faithfully following Him in that venture. These promises aren't meant to just be add-ons to our own individual pursuits. Christianity is following Christ and His promises to us are for us in that following of Him.

All believers have callings, a mission, and will be given specific tasks. This isn't something only reserved for missionaries, pastors, or other ministry vocations. This is the truth for every believer.

You have a calling.

You have a mission.

You will be or have been given specific assignments.

The president of Gateway Seminary, Jeff Iorg, has written one of the most insightful books on one's calling, *Is God Calling Me?* It's a small book, but a must-read for any believer, especially someone wrestling with a call to vocational ministry. In his book,

Iorg provides a tool to help visualize what is meant by one's calling. We wanted to provide it to you, to help you reflect on what your life calling may be. It's helpful to identify your potential calling(s) and specific God-given missions before taking the 40-day trek.

That tool is listed below, but first, here's Iorg's definition of a calling; "A call is a profound impression from God that establishes parameters for your life and can be altered only by a subsequent, superseding impression from God."[11]

For something that is hard to define, this definition is as good as it gets. It's hard to put into words. The idea is that, in how every way the Holy Spirit has revealed direction in your life, He does so to a degree that trumps all else that has been revealed to you. And this direction is always within the bounds of Scripture. That distinct revelation then forms parameters or boundaries to your life, expressing the direction you should go and not go. Callings and specific assignments may change, but that change should only come when a conviction as profound as the original comes upon our own lives.

Here is the diagram that Iorg provides and we relay to you as a tool:

$$\{\,[\,(\,\text{YOUR LIFE}\,)\,]\,\}$$

The brackets represent the parameters that a call and mission set for your life. We receive different levels of calls. First,

---

[11] Iorg, Jeff. *Is God Calling Me?: Answering the Question Every Believer Asks*. Nashville, Tenn: B&H Publishing Group, 2008.

all believers have a general call. That's a call unto salvation which leads to a call to follow Christ and make disciples. Our lives are all bound to this calling. It's represented by the first bracket.

{ = General Call of the Believer

Second, is a call to an area of ministry. Iorg describes it as ministry leadership, but that should be expanded to any area of ministry. This is represented by the second bracket.

[= Specific Call to Ministry

Third, is that within our general call to follow and make disciples, as well as our call to an area of ministry, we receive particular tasks and assignments. This is where the most frequent change will come. This is represented by the parenthesis.

(= Specific Task or Assignment within Your Call

The goal of this tool being provided is so you can work through your calling and mission. Then prayerfully seek the Lord concerning them as you read the daily devotionals. A blank diagram is going to be provided for you, but first I have shared one from my personal life to help explain this exercise.

Jake's Callings for Example

{ [(YOUR LIFE)] }

A specific task to teach my kids about missionaries, pastor the church I pastor, and write this book.

A call to be a husband, father, pastor, and write.

My general call to follow and make disciples.

{ [(YOUR LIFE)] }

_____

_____

_____

INVINCIBLE PRAYER MATRIX

When it Seems God isn't Giving the Victory, Provision, or Protection isn't Happening

In the introduction and throughout the chapters, a disclaimer is consistently being made, which is that the invincibility, victory, provision, or protection is only guaranteed by God's promises when we're trying to faithfully follow Him. Again, that doesn't mean God doesn't give victories, provide, or protect His people when they are off the path. He often does. So much so that it's hard to determine if this disclaimer is true. When He does that, He is providing through His grace and mercy.

Think of our lives like the Israelites in the campaigns of conquest found in the book of Joshua. When they sought God and obeyed Him, they won dominant victories. When they went on their own power and were disobedient, they were severely defeated.

There really needs to be a label like many products have: "For best results use as directed." For best results of God-given invincibility, seek Him, follow Him, and obey Him. Be in His Will.

But even when we're seeking Him and completely obedient, we can feel as if He is not keeping His promises. We

203

can feel vulnerable instead of invincible. Events in our lives may feel like He's not giving us victory, provision, or protection. Sometimes this feeling is because we're just not seeing the provision, but other times it may be withheld.

The list below is intended to be a prayer matrix for you to use to pray through those times. A list of possible reasons has been provided, along with Scripture references. To use this matrix, read the possible reasons and Scripture references, then in your prayer time, just ask the Lord about each of them. If one of these is the case, the Holy Spirit may make you aware of it, but know there are also occasions when it's just not the time for explanation or understanding. Continue in faith, God hasn't ever failed His people.

- **Sin** – (John 1:4–9) The first stop in this matrix is to assess yourself, and you don't have to look too far in this case. Is there sin you are intentionally or continually committing? God isn't going to work in the midst of that disobedience. There are times He will show mercy and grace, but don't let that keep you from confessing that sin, repenting, and leaving that sin in the dust.

- **So Many Would Be Saved** – (2 Peter 3:9) Our chief calling is to make disciples and that should be our greatest desire. Therefore, the salvation of others trumps all our needs. This is the greatest good God can be doing on our behalf. Could the seeming lack of provision be that God is at work so others might be saved?

- **Mercy** – (Romans 9:15) Provision and protection is relative. There's no set level that we're promised. Maintaining a particular level of standard of living isn't the bar for whether God is truly providing or protecting us. Sometimes He does allow provision and protection that far outweighs the minimum need. We must realize that God shows mercy and blessings to whom He wants. Our level of provision isn't promised to be the same as someone else. We should not compare. In fact, God has already shown us the greatest mercy when Jesus died for our sins. Could God be asking us to trust Him in a difficult circumstance?

- **Discipline** – (Hebrews 12:4–12) This is always the most likely scenario in which we seemingly take a loss or feel like provision isn't happening. God is shaping us into who we need to be. This discipline isn't meant to be punishment, though it can be at times. Often, it's for our growth, maturing, preparation, or shaping. Could God be disciplining you? Could God be growing you?

- **Greater Good** – (Isaiah 55:8–9) Always there is a larger picture we don't see. God can see it. Your seeming lack of provision could be because God is working for a greater good. Could God be working a greater good through your difficulty?

- **Protecting from a Greater Evil** – (Isaiah 55:8–9) Just as there is a greater good in which God could be working

205

towards through our situation, He could also be saving us from a much worse situation. Could God be sparing you from something worse?

- **Not Seeking Him** – (Matthew 6:33) His promise for provision comes as we seek Him first. Are you seeking Him?

- **Not on the Altar** – (Romans 12:1) His promise of provision and protection is for us when we surrender our life to Him and follow Him. The image of laying ourselves on the altar and then not being able to provide for or protect ourselves gives the imagery of how this promise of invincibility works.

- **Not Where He Wants** – (Isaiah 14:27 & Job 42:2) This is just another way of looking at the past two points. Have you been following Him? Are you where He wants you to be? And if the answer is no, ask Him where you need to be. Then adjust and ask Him to help you be where He wants you.

- **Not Asking** – (Matthew 7:7–8) This seems too obvious, but it happens, just as this verse says you have not because you ask not. Ask Him for victory, provision, or protection that is needed.

- **Humbling** – (1 Peter 5:6) "Discipline" above touches on this. Part of our maturity and growth is being humbled.

206

We need to look at this especially in terms of provision and victory. God wants us to be humble, realizing our need for Him.

- **Not in His Will** – (Isaiah 14:27 & Job 42:2) This has been worded in different ways—not seeking, not on the altar, or not where the Lord wants us, but we need to also realize God has a plan. We have to be in tune with Him to know where we need to be in relation to that plan.

- **Moved Past His Protection** – (James 1:14–15) While in the wilderness, the Israelites followed the pillar of fire and smoke. They were under God's protection and provision while they were behind or under that pillar. If they advanced ahead, then they were in a dangerous zone. We can't run faster than God wants us to run.

- **Made Own Way** – (Isaiah 50:10–11) It's tempting to not wait on God's provision or protection, but to make our own way. Has your own way caused the trouble you're in?

- **We're ALWAYS protected from the Second Death** – (Revelation 20:6) We must realize that the ultimate protection is salvation.

Appendix 4

ATTRIBUTES OF GOD

We're Invincible Because God is Invincible

This devotional book is meant to increase your confidence in God. There are three main ways in which this can happen. The first is by studying the attributes or characteristics of God. This is a large part of Systematic Theology, a discipline that takes the whole counsel of Scripture and builds a composite picture of God. This straightforwardly states who God is and what God can do. The second is by studying the works of God in Scripture and history. Reading and reflecting on what God has done in the past shows us who He is and what He can do. The third is by personally experiencing God working in your own life. This is where the knowledge from Scripture takes on life, and it is personally seen and felt in our own lives.

This book focuses on the second method—looking at the feats God has done in the past. But to help provide even more support in building your confidence in God, we're providing a list of characteristics of God. It's far from exhaustive, but it focuses on the attributes directly related to victory, provision, and protection.

Attributes of the Invincible God

Omnipotent .... He's all-powerful

Omnipresent .... He's all-present

Omniscient .... He's all-knowing

Eternal .... He will always be

Infinite .... He has always been and always will be

Triune .... He is one in essence, three in persons

Creator .... He made all

Sovereign .... He's over all

Self-sustaining .... He needs nothing

Holy .... He's set apart

Transcendent .... He's beyond all

Unchangeable .... He is the same now as in the past

Wise .... He always executes the right judgment

Victorious .... He wins all

Sustainer .... He holds all

Limitless .... He's without limitations

Provider .... He meets our needs

Capable .... He's more than able

Faithful .... He keeps His word

Protector .... He keeps us from harm

A Fortress .... He protects us

A Shield .... He protects us

A Refuge .... He is a safe place

Caring .... He knows and cares about our lives

Love .... He loves us

Good .... He is and always does good

Patient .... He is slow to anger

Appendix 5

WORKS OF GOD

We're Invincible Because God is Invincible.

Each of the forty devotions included an account of God's work recorded in the Bible or in history. Only forty were chosen, but of course, there are way more recorded in Scripture and much more recorded in the journals of God's people. To provide another resource to help you build confidence in Him, a list of those accounts is provided. Blanks have also been provided in Appendix 6, so that you can list more that are impactful to you.

Works of the Invincible God

1. *God Giving David Victory Over Goliath - from 1 Samuel 17*
2. *God Rescuing Israel from Egypt - from Exodus 1–14*
3. *God Giving Israel Victory Over Jericho - from Joshua 5:13–6:27*
4. *God Giving Samson Victory Over a Thousand - from Judges 15*

23. *God Creating Everything - from Genesis 1 & 2*

24. *God Giving a Proof of Healing to Hezekiah - from 2 Kings 20*

25. *God Bringing the Savior into the World - from Luke 1 & 2*

26. *Jesus Walking on the Water - from Mark 6*

27. *Jesus Raising Lazarus from the Dead - from John 11*

28. *God Making your Impossible Challenge Possible - from Your Life*

29. *God Providing for Taxes - from Matthew 17*

30. *God Protecting and Empowering the First Christians - from Acts*

31. *God Bringing Paul to Rome - from Acts 20–27*

32. *God Protecting Polycarp from Flames - from History*

33. *God Providing for George Mueller - from History*

34. *God Saving the Waodani Tribe - from Modern History*

35. *God Working in the World Today - from Current Events*

36. *God Keeping His Promise to Preserve Israel - from Revelation 12*

37. *Jesus Defeating the Antichrist - from Revelation 19*

38. *Jesus Ruling and Defeating Satan at the End of the Millennial Kingdom - from Revelation 20*

39. *God Dwelling with His people Again - from Revelation 21*

40. *Jesus Walking with You - from Revelation 1*

Appendix 6

EXPERIENCE

We're Invincible Because God is Invincible.

This appendix is a blank list ready for you to complete to show how God has already worked in your life. We've read that He works in His people beyond the Bible. Chances are, He has already given you victories, provision, protection, and made the impossible possible. Use this resource to record and remember how He has worked in your life.

Works of the Invincible God in Your Life

1. _____

2. _____

3. _____

4. _____

5. _____

6. _____

7. _____

8. _____

9. _____

10. _____

11. _____

12. _____

13. _____

14. _____

15. _____

16. _____

17. _____

18. _____

19. _____

20. _____

21. _____

22. _____

23. _____

24. _____

25. _____

26. _____

27. _____

28. _____

29. _____

30. _____

31. _____

32. _____

33. _____

34. _____

35. _____

36. _____

37. _____

38. _____

39. _____

40. _____

Appendix 7

ENCOURAGEMENT VERSES

In Christ, You're invincible

Each of the forty devotions included an encouragement verse. Only forty were chosen, but of course, there are way more in Scripture. To provide you with another resource to help build confidence in God, a list of these verses has been provided. In Appendix 8, a blank list has been provided so that you can record more that are impactful to you.

Encouragement Verses

1. *Even though I walk through the darkest valley, I will fear no evil, for you are with me; your rod and your staff, they comfort me (Psalm 23:4, NIV).*
2. *He [God] rescued me from my powerful enemy, from my foes, who were too strong for me (Psalm 18:17, NIV).*
3. *With your help I can advance against a troop; with my God I can scale a wall (Psalm 18:29, NIV).*

4. *You armed me with strength for battle; you humbled my adversaries before me (Psalm 18:39, NIV).*

5. *I will not fear though tens of thousands assail me on every side (Psalm 3:6, NIV).*

6. *He will swallow up death forever; and the Lord God will wipe away tears from all faces, and the reproach of His people He will take away from all the earth, for the Lord has spoken (Isaiah 25:8, ESV).*

7. *Surely, I am with you always, to the very end of the age (Matthew 28:20, NIV).*

8. *The lions may grow weak and hungry, but those who seek the Lord lack no good thing (Psalm 34:10, NIV).*

9. *My eyes are ever on the LORD, for only He will release my feet from the snare (Psalm 25:15, NIV).*

10. *Since You are my rock and my fortress, for the sake of Your Name lead and guide me. Keep me free from the trap that is set for me, for You are my refuge (Psalms 31:3–4, NIV).*

11. *For the pagans run after all these things, and your heavenly Father knows that you need them (Matthew 6:32, NIV).*

12. *Some trust in chariots and some in horses, but we trust in the name of the Lord our God. They are brought to their knees and fall, but we rise up and stand firm (Psalm 20:7–8, NIV).*

13. *"Which of you, if your son asks for bread, will give him a stone? Or if he asks for a fish, will give him a snake? If you, then, though you are evil, know how to give good gifts to your children, how much more will your Father in heaven give good gifts to those who ask Him! (Matthew 7:9–11, NIV).*

14. "So Abraham called the name of that place, 'The LORD will provide'; as it is said to this day, 'On the mount of the LORD it shall be provided'" (Genesis 28:22:14, ESV).
15. Save me from the mouth of the lion! You have rescued me from the horns of the wild oxen! (Psalm 22:21, ESV).
16. My eyes are ever on the Lord, for only He will release my feet from the snare (Psalm 25:15, NIV).
17. No one who hopes in You will ever be put to shame... (Psalm 25:3a, NIV).
18. As for God, His way is perfect: The Lord's word is flawless; He shields all who take refuge in Him (Psalm 34:10, NIV).
19. I will fear no evil, for You are with me... (Psalm 23:4, NIV).
20. "Who is this? Even the wind and the waves obey Him!" (Mark 4:41, NIV).
21. For in the day of trouble He will keep me safe in His dwelling; He will hide me in the shelter of His sacred tent and set me high upon a rock (Psalm 27:5, NIV).
22. Though an army besiege me, my heart will not fear; though war break out against me, even then I will be confident (Psalm 27:3, NIV).
23. The earth is the Lord's, and everything in it, the world, and all who live in it (Psalm 24:1, NIV).
24. Great is our Lord and mighty in power; His understanding has no limit (Psalm 147:5, NIV).
25. "For nothing will be impossible with God" (Luke 1:37, ESV).
26. Our help is in the name of the LORD, the Maker of heaven and earth (Psalm 24:1, NIV).

27. *And we know that in all things God works for the good of those who love Him, who have been called according to His purpose (Romans 8:28, ESV).*

28. *Surely Your goodness and love will follow me all the days of my life, and I will dwell in the house of the Lord forever (Psalm 23:6, NIV).*

29. *Is anything too hard for the Lord? (Genesis 18:14, NIV).*

30. *Many are saying of me, "God will not deliver him." But You, Lord, are a shield around me, my glory, the One who lifts my head high (Psalm 3:2–3, NIV).*

31. *When the wicked advance against me to devour me, it is my enemies and my foes who will stumble and fall (Psalm 27:2, NIV).*

32. *I called to the Lord, who is worthy of praise, and I have been saved from my enemies (Psalm 18:3, NIV).*

33. *It is my eager expectation and hope that I will not be at all ashamed, but that with full courage now as always Christ will be honored in my body, whether by life or by death. For to me to live is Christ, and to die is gain (Philippians 1:20-21, ESV).*

34. *In this world you will have trouble. But take heart! I have overcome the world" (John 16:33, NIV).*

35. *To Him who is able to keep you from stumbling and to present you before His glorious presence without fault and with great joy (Jude 1:24, NIV).*

36. *Keep me as the apple of Your eye; hide me in the shadow of Your wings from the wicked who are out to destroy me, from my mortal enemies who surround me (Psalm 17:8–9, NIV).*

37. *We wait for the blessed hope—the appearing of the glory of our great God and Savior, Jesus Christ (Titus 2:13, NIV).*

38. *Do not be afraid. I am the First and the Last. I am the Living One; I was dead, and now look, I am alive for ever and ever! And I hold the keys of death and Hades (Revelation 1:17–18, NIV).*

39. *For our light and momentary troubles are achieving for us an eternal glory that far outweighs them all. So we fix our eyes not on what is seen, but on what is unseen, since what is seen is temporary, but what is unseen is eternal (2 Corinthians 4:17–18, NIV).*

40. *I can do all things through Christ who strengthens me (Philippians 4:13, NKJV).*

Appendix 8

We're Invincible Because God is Invincible

This appendix is a blank list ready for you to complete by listing verses that encourage and remind you that through Christ, you're invincible. These verses may be about the character of God, His abilities, His victories, His provision, His protection, Him making the impossible possible, or anything else that encourages you to follow Him in obedience.

Additional Invincible Encouragement Verses

1. _____

2. _____

3. _____

4. _____

5. _____

6. _____

7. _____

8. _____

9. _____

10. _____

11. _____

12. _____

13. _____

14. _____

15. _____

16. _____

17. _____

18. _____

19. _____

20. _____

21. _____

22. _____

23. _____

24. _____

25. _____

26. _____

27. _____

28. _____

29. _____

30. _____

31. _____

32. _____

33. _____

34. _____

35. _____

36. _____

37. _____

38. _____

39. _____

40. _____

Did you enjoy the 40-day journey of *Invincible?*
You can make it an annual journey.

Each Lent, a new spiritual preparedness
devotional book will be released!

Devotional Book #2

Circa Regna Tonat: A 40-Day journey through
the Exilic Prophets to strengthen faith in a chaotic world.

RELEASES
FEB. 12, 2020

Register for an alert at:
www.standfirmministries.com/spiritualpreparednessdevotionals

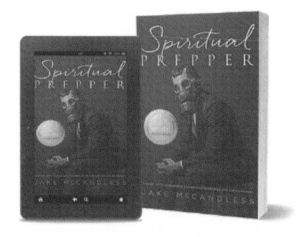

The award-winning book
that laid the foundation for *Invincible*.

AVAILABLE
NOW

where all books are sold.

Find this and other resources at:
www.spiritualprepperstore.com

The next release from Stand Firm Books.
An intro to what we all must prepare to face.

RELEASES
JAN. 1, 2020

where all books are sold.

Register for an alert at:
www.standfirmministries.com/readyornot

Introducing Spiritual Warrior
Resources & Groups

Sorority of Spiritual Warriors &
Fraternity of Spiritual Warriors

COMING
SOON

*Register for alerts and updates
at www.standfirmministries.com/spiritualwarrior.*

Devotional Book for Women by Dr. Angela Ruark
&
Devotional Book for Men by
Jake McCandless & Roland Dunkerley

Children know Jesus in the manger
and on the cross,
but do they know Him on the white horse?

COMING SOON

Register for alerts and updates at:
www.standfirmministries.com/prophecysimplifiedforkids.

Made in the USA
Coppell, TX
05 February 2020

15457048R00146